CBI and Policing in India

From Vedic Period to Modern Times

Devi Dayal Aggarwal

Foreword by

K.P.S. Gill

2000

Kaveri Books

New Delhi - 110 002

First Published in 2000

ISBN 81-7479-034-9

Published by : **Rakesh Goel**
Kaveri Books
4697/5-21-A, Ansari Road,
New Delhi - 110002 (India).
Tel : 328 8140 Fax : 011-7198902
e.mail : kaveribooks@vsnl.com

Printed at : **Chawla Offset Printers, Delhi-110052**

Computer Graphics : **Akshar Computer Kendra, Delhi-110085**

Printed in India

FOREWORD

At this moment of time, there is criticism of all police forces right across the world, on grounds of prejudice or violation of human rights and inability to meet the needs of the people. However, till date, we have not been able to create any viable alternatives or methods required to restrain the various stresses and strains that exist within society, which if unchecked, could only lead to chaos. Policing society has been one of the basic functions of governance in all societies of the world. Through the course of history, we discover that the measure of an efficient society lies in the efficiency of its security network, in its police forces. As one of the oldest civilizations in the world, the history and culture of India reveal a highly evolved and ordered society. The patterns and methods of governance operated at highly sophisticated levels; levels which took the West hundreds of years to reach. Yet, the generally held belief, is one that the Britishers were responsible for the creation of a modern police force in India.

It is misplaced beliefs, such as these, that the author lays bare, while highlighting many other significant aspects, which were hitherto unknown. In this book, the author traces the history of policing down the ages in India. We discover that throughout Indian history we have observed a tradition wherein protection of the life and property of the people had been the cardinal function of the State. A complex system involving a network of spies, who provided vital information to the rulers, has been in existence through the ages. Evidence of this can be found in ancient texts and tracts dealing with statecraft. The system of policing, devised by the British for India was based on their own experience as a colonial power. While taking in mind the unique Indian conditions, the system was put in place after a wide ranging debate within the administrators of that time and surprisingly, a real effort was made to ensure that the police force did not become oppressive or exploitative.

The CBI began as a special police establishment within the police and its charter was to investigate cases involving corruption within the establishment. As pressures on the special force increased, the need was felt for a central police agency at the disposal of the Central Government, whose brief would extend beyond mere investigation of corruption cases. Thus, the present day CBI was created, and today it is performing a variety of tasks relating not only to corruption but also to the security of the State.

While we can trace the historical processes of the evolution of policing structures in ancient India, in the present era, sadly, we have very little current writings on the police. There is little by way of literature, which is based on study and research, what ever exists are mere media fulminations on the lapses and failures of the police. However, it is heartening that scholars are now coming forward and bringing out meaningful books on the police. The present book, which deals with the CBI and investigative agencies within the police, is an important contribution to this literature and field. Today, the CBI is one of the premier agencies in the country. There is tremendous regard for its professionalism and its impartiality, and from time to time demands are made by political parties as well as people in general to entrust difficult and sensitive cases to the CBI. The danger here is that the force is fast becoming over-burdened and in comparison with similar agencies in advanced countries, is still under-equipped and under-manned.

In this context, it must be noted that it is only when the people and media realize—and force those, who control political and executive power in this country to realize—that the force must be empowered, must be continuously upgraded, trained, equipped and retrained, if it is to be effective against the unflagging innovations of criminal enterprise, that these trends may be reversed. And realize also that one of the most fruitful and most productive investments that a nation can make is that of upholding law and order—for without these, all other investments will, in time, be lost to strife. It is after all, not coincidental that a powerful nation is built on the backbone of the twin forces of strong law keeping and efficient intelligence gathering. That the reverse also holds true, and has been historically proven, is one of the major insights.

Mr. D.D. Aggarwal provides in this volume "CBI and Policing" which traces the history of intelligence and law enforcement.

(K.P.S. Gill)

CONTENTS

Foreword *iii*
Introduction *ix*

1. Rajdharma (Duties of a Raja) 1
2. Vedic Period 6
3. Ramayana Period 17
4. Krishna Period 31
5. Maurya Period to Rajput Period 38
6. Mohammedan Period 60
7. British Period and Thereafter 73
8. Conclusion 101

Resolution 109
Annexure 110
Glossary 114
Index 116

INTRODUCTION

Central Bureau of Investigations (CBI) and Policing in India is said to be the creation of British rule in India. I came across some such connotation and started working on it to find its genesis and to see if it was the creation of British in India, then how our ancient rulers had been managing the governance of vast empires, particularly during the periods of Mauryas, Guptas and Mughals.

On searching the ancient literature, vedas and smritis, I found that a lot has been said about these aspects in our granthas, particularly the Arthshastra of Chanakya (Kautilya) recognised world over. One thing, however, is there that in ancient period the CBI and various Police organisations were combined in the spies and the organisation for the protection of life and property of the people. The protection of life and property of the people from foreign aggression and internal criminals was the bestowed job of the raja according to the functional division of the mankind by Manu into four varnas—Brahmin, Kshatriya, Vaish and Shudra. Brahmins were responsible for learning and teaching, Kshatriyas for ruling the country with a view to protecting the life and property of the people from external aggressions and internal criminals as also to think of the well-being of the subjects; Vaishas were entrusted with the job of trade, agriculture, grazing, industry and Shudras were to serve the people of other three varnas to enable them to discharge their duties religiously.

In our granthas, the duties entrusted to individuals had been considered as their dharma so that a sanctity is attached to it by virtue of which the persons would discharge their duties ungrudgingly and with their best effort e.g. the discharge of the duties by a raja was called 'Rajdharma' and so on. In the discharge of his duty of proper governance, the raja had to take help of the spies and other persons responsible for maintenance of law and order, catching the criminals, handing them over to the Magistrates for getting them punished so that they did not resort to such malpractices in future. The spies were engaged in the country and abroad and they were directly responsible to the raja to apprise him about the happenings in the country and abroad in favour or against the rajya. Same jobs continue to be done by the present organisation of CBI and other Police—Central and State—organisations. It is, therefore, more than certain that there has been a proper CBI and Police organisation in our ancient period as also during the Mohammedan rule in India followed by British rule. May be it has continued to be adopted as per Arthshastra.

This aspect has been narrated in this book tracing the history of 'Policing and CBI' right from the Vedas to date. It will be of interest and educative to all, particularly those in these organisations.

D.D. Aggarwal

1 RAJDHARMA (Duties of a Raja)

Since the jobs of spying and maintenance of law and order pertain to Rajdharma, it is better to discuss the duties of a raja as per ancient granthas. After preliminary studies under the guru, the students used to proceed further in the study of vocational efficiency. A student having interest in further studies, became a Brahmin, responsible for maintenance of dharma in the rajya and teaching the individuals. A student having taste in warfare, was educated in fighting, and rajniti and became Kshatriya. Similarly, the student having interest in trade etc. was trained in trade, agriculture, industry and became Vaish. A person, who could not fit in any of the above three vocations, adopted the varna of Shudra. Since each person had then adopted the varna as per his capability/interest, none had grudge in having adopted a particular varna.

Duties of a raja as per vedic and samritis' tenets are as under :

1. The need for a raja was felt as per evolution of state. With the advent of mankind, the persons at first became a family under the head of the family; then it became a society and then a community followed by the creation of a rajya under the raja. The mightiest person, able to protect the people and their property was elected or became the raja and for maintaining the law and order and protection from aggression by other rajas, he had to maintain an army and had to raise funds for meeting the expenses of the army and his household out of the products in the state.

2. The raja should be quick in solving problems of people and the state and providing peace and prosperity to his people.

3. He should have tours incognito so that he is able to know what is happening in the state.
4. He should arrange for proper education of his subjects so that there is none illiterate.
5. He should be very brave so that he is able to defeat the enemies.
6. He should appreciate the works done by gentleman.
7. He should be able to keep his exchequer filled with money.
8. He should have a net of spies so that he is able to collect all that is going on in his kingdom and in other countries concerning him.
9. He should be protector of all dharmas and see that people of all varnas act according to the tenets of their respective dharmas.
10. He should have proper force to maintain law and order; catch the criminals and award them suitable punishment.
11. He should maintain properly equipped army to protect the kingdom from external aggressions.
12. He should always think of the well-being of his people; provide all comforts like construction of roads, provision of gardens and sarais all along the roads and assure fear-free travel.
13. He should perform yagyas from time to time so that all gods are happy and ensure timely rains, good crops, etc.
14. He should provide hospitals etc. to ensure ailments-free life.
15. He should fix reasonable percentage of product to be remitted to raja's exchequer for meeting the cost of running the governance.
16. The wealth so collected should be spent on maintenance of army, as also on the welfare works of his people.

17. He should be very kind-hearted and respectful to all elders and benevolent to others.

18. He should see that justice is provided to the aggrieved persons in courts under him and no culprit goes unpunished.

19. He should arrange relief to public when there is no rain and there is famine.

20. He should hold Aswamedha yagyas to establish his suzerainty on the vassal states.

21. He should fix prices of essential commodities so that the same are available to laymen at reasonable prices and also control weights and measures so that there is no cheating in these and the culprits are suitably punished.

22. He should be well-versed with the warfare manipulations, dealing with the other rajas, fighting with the enemies and execution of proper agreements with the defeated rajas. He should also be well-versed with laws of war, laws of peace, etc.

23. In Ram Rajya, Raja Ram had gone to the extent of advising his people the way of attaining salvation although, as accepted by Ram himself, it was only an advice and was not binding on the people, who could act as per their volition.

24. As per Platonic theory, as propounded by vedic tenets also, the Rajdharma should be above all self interests. Plato goes to the extent of providing that king should not have wife and children so that he does not develop any self-interest.

25. The raja should have the Sabha or Samiti or Council of Ministers, advisors to advise him on all important matters and the raja should abide by that advice or else should advance reasons for not accepting the same.

26. The raja should be above all sensuous excesses so that his character is followed by his subjects too.

27. The raja should construct unaccessible forts for the security of the rajya in case of invasion and these forts should be properly protected by strong army. There should be sufficient stock of foodgrains, provision for water etc. for the army in case the fort is beseized.

28. The raja should have a proper system of distribution of the booty obtained from the defeated Rajas, amongst his exchequer and the army and commanders so that the army and commanders could be kept in good humour and are always faithful to the raja.

29. The raja should divide his kingdom in divisions, sub-divisions and villages. Each village to have its Panchayat with one Mukhiya; then there should be a block of ten village under another Pradhan; then another Pradhan of twenty villages, then of one hundred villages and then one governor for one thousand villages. Each division should have the governors of confidence to be kept under constant vigil. Each town too should have a Council like the present day Municipality. These Panchayats and Councils were responsible for the maintenance of law and order in their respective areas and doing all jobs of well-being of the people. Also they should report the short-comings, shortage of commodities, position of crime etc in each village, block of villages and towns to enable the raja to take appropriate action in remedying the same.

30. Further proper vigil should be there on the Government employees so that they do not resort to corrupt practices and such corrupt people, when detected, should be severely punished. Therefore, at the time of appointment of such people, it should be seen that they are capable, are from high class families and with good reputation. Their conduct should be got verified by independent means before such appointment. Such Government employees should be adequately paid so that they do not resort to corrupt practices.

31. Apart from share of agricultural product, the raja can

impose professional tax, trade tax, customs cess to raise money for the exchequer.

32. All materials under the ground belong to the raja. The raja should, therefore, arrange proper protection of mines and their exploitation so that these are not taken away by the people unauthorisedly.

33. In the end, the raja should be handsome, with impressive personality, well-dressed, brave, intelligent and benevolent but very strict in dealing with the criminals.

34. After ruling for the period till he became ripe for proceeding for vanprastha, the raja should hand over the rajya to his successors and go to forests without looking back to his family etc. This was necessary to provide a chance to the grown up sons to handle the governance lest they, out of their temptation to rule, should oust the raja creating an awkward position as Aurangzeb had put Shahjahan, his father, in jail till he died there in solitude.

2 VEDIC PERIOD

The term Police connotes the purposeful maintenance of public order and protection of persons from the hazards of public accidents and the commission of unlawful acts. It applies to the body of civil officers charged with maintaining public order and safety and enforcing the law including the prevention and detection of crime.

Western scholars unanimously hold the view that the Indian Police and CBI system is a creation of British rule in India. It has, however, been conceded that from the vedic period, the changing pattern of governments, notwithstanding, the protection of life and property of the people, has been the cardinal function of the state. It is, however, difficult to isolate references to Police organisation in ancient Indian polity as the mention of different forms of crimes administration of criminal justice and the structure of internal security system, are inextricably linked with the broad stream of religion, ethics and political institutions. They, however, failed to appreciably understand and analyse the origin and development of law enforcement institutions in ancient India since the Western Police organisations themselves cannot be traced to antiquity.

From the duties of the raja, as enunciated in vedas and shastras, indicated in previous chapter, it would be observed that the main jobs of the raja revolve around the system of policing, army and spying. The maintenance of law and order in the country and protection of people from foreign aggression, locating and getting the criminals punished are the main jobs for which the institution of governance and the raja were created.

We have evidence of the existence of security organisation in Harappan civilisation. The Indus people had established trading stations all along the coast so that their ships sailing on high seas could be refurbished and drawn ashore in time of distress. The early vedic samritis elaborately illustrate the insecure living conditions of the pastoral vedic community, who constantly beseached the celestical deities to protect them and their material belongings, not only from natural calamities but also from human marauders. The vedas and brahminas are replete with prayers on this score. There is hardly any crime, which was not known then on account of which the vedic people lived restless and nightmarish at times. Varuna is the earliest known prototype of the all powerful ubiquitous policeman, who monitored and controlled the lives of the people and ensured their security and general well-being. Even in Budhist and Jain canonical literature, there is mention of ocean going ships and trading caravans carrying security men with them.

Vedas and samritis are the granthas in existence eversince the advent of mankind. These granthas provide for the duties of the people of all varnas. The raja had the specially prescribed duties as his conduct was responsible for the well-being of his subjects. In vedas, Indra has been presented as a raja and the other gods, Varuna, Agni, Sun, Aswanikumar are his ministers to help him in the governance of the country. Here Indra and other gods, Varuna etc. are not to be treated as the raja of Swarga etc. but symbolise the raja of the universe or a country with his team of ministers. In this way, full structure of the governance has been provided in vedas. Varuna etc. have been entrusted with the monitoring of their respective departments as assistants of the raja, as in present days, there is a President and Council of Ministers but all Ministers and bureaucrats act on behalf of the President so much so that they even issue orders "for and on behalf of the President" and are thus mini Presidents within themselves.

In the distribution of portfolios, Agni is the Minister-incharge of the ambassadors, spies and Varuna is the Minister-incharge of Police Department. Varuna is presented as a friend of Raja Indra as well. Varuna has been made incharge of Police because in vedas, Varuna has been mentioned with 'handcuff', tie-bonds etc. and that is the job of the police e.g. handcuffing the culprits.

ये ते पाशा वरुण सप्त सप्त त्रेधा तिष्ठन्ति विषिता स्वान्तः।
सिनन्तु सर्वे अनृतं यः सत्यवाधति तं सृजन्तु।।

Meaning that Varuna has three kinds of handcuffs for arresting the culprits of three types—very hardened criminals, ordinary criminals and casual criminals. Also, Varuna is directed to arrest such criminals and leave the gentlemen. In this way, the job of Varuna is to arrest the criminals and leave the gentlemen and this exactly is the job of Police at present too. A very tough handcuff is provided to arrest the hardened criminals and then milder for arresting the other types of criminals. Then to get them punished, commensurately as per their crime, is also the job of the police. It shows that in our samritis there is proper description of all crimes and there would have been a penal code like our present day Indian Penal Code, Criminal Procedure Code etc. so much so that Varuna even gets a person punished when he rebukes someone so that the people are truth-abiding. It is also the duty of Varuna to investigate the crime so that the reality is known and the guilty only is punished. Then only he arrests and presents before the Magistrate. It shows that in our vedas too it has been an accepted principal that the Police, who arrests the criminal and the Magistrate, who awards punishment, are distinct persons.

Along with Varuna, there is also the mention of his spies in Chapter IV of Atharva Veda. Here there is mention of the spies and then the system of arresting the criminals.

1. Varun has many eyes so that he is able to see every person doing his job. In other words, Varuna, with the assistance of his spies, is available in every nook and corner to see the activities of the people so as to find the wrong-doers.
2. The men of Varuna also look into the cheats, thieves, teasers and those, who plan such activities sitting in isolated places. They then follow them secretly and catch them so that they are not successful in their mission.

In this way there is a fear in the mind of everyone lest he too might be caught by Varuna's men.

3. Varuna being incharge of law and order on this land, he comes to know of what is happening here. What to speak of the activities on land, Varun comes to know of what is happening under the sea or in space.

4. The spies of Varuna are posted over entire land. They are very alert and vigilant and come to know of the minutest happenings.

In this way, there is a detailed narration of the duties of Varuna, the Police Minister, in vedas. There is a chain of the Varuna's spies and they are present in every nook and corner and watch every activity on earth, under the sea and in space. They arrest the criminals, get them punished and arrange to put them behind the bars. In other words the activities of Varuna or Police include finding out the criminals, arresting them, getting them punished by competent authority and after conviction put them behind the bars. These exactly are the jobs of Police at present too. Varuna, therefore, has to be very alert, vigilant and keep a watch on his surroundings. His qualities are :

(i) Alertness (जागृवांसा (ऋग० 1-136-3)

(ii) Vigilant (विचर्षणी (ऋग० 5-63-3)

(iii) With thousand eyes (क्षहस्त्र चक्षा (ऋग० 7-34-10)

It shows that the men of Varuna would be expert in seeing the people, knowing them and recognising them from the angle of their conduct.

In Rig Veda, Varun has been addressed as 'विश्वस्य प्रचेतसा' (5-71-2) i.e. a person, who warns everyone to keep alert. It also shows that Varuna's men in the first instance warn the ill-doers to be careful and not to re-occur the bad deed and if he still continues to remain on wrong path, he is arrested and got punished. It is a very good reformist idea if a criminal could be set right on issuing warning only initially. Varuna also appreciates the people on right path and he continuously preaches people to keep aside from the wrong-doings. Varuna is accordingly also called 'सत्पती' (Truth-lover), शुभस्पती (Well-wisher) धर्मणा–व्रहा (Religious) etc. Varuna, therefore, is benevolent to the people on right path and is very strict towards the criminals, and enemies. It is only because of the alertness of Varuna and his men, that the people live safe and secure and do all their jobs without any fear.

Whenever any person comes to Varuna or his men with any complaint to be redressed, he listens to the same immediately and tries to remove the grievance. He is, therefore, called well-wisher of all.

It has been indicated above that spies have a special relation with Varuna. Also there is mention in vedas that Indra, Agni, Soma etc had their own spies. This must be correct as apart from the centralised spies organisation, each Department would be having their own spies too to keep them informed about the happenings pertaining to their Departments such as a Revenue Minister would keep a watch that no one evades payment of dues of the rajya etc. that is why the speciality of the spies has been indicated wherever there is mention of the spies of other Departments e.g.:

1. The raja is expected to know through his personal men of confidence (working as spies) to see if the enemy has any designs against him or in public too if anyone is planning to revolt etc. so that such elements are suppressed before they take ugly shape. (Rig 4-4-3)
2. In this way the subjects, howsoever strong and rich, they may become, they cannot go against the order of the raja as the spies of raja would immediately inform the raja of any such voice coming up and would suppress the same. (Rig 1-33-8)
3. At the same time all Ministers entrust the spying job to Varuna too because they know that the spies of Varuna could bring any information from anywhere. (Rig 6-67-5)
4. The raja's spies keep on wandering on land, in fields,

in trade centres and at places of public gatherings. They protect the righteous persons and detect and arrest the ill-designers. (Rig 7-61-3)

5. The spies have to keep on moving as they have to detect the criminals and get them punished. They would not be performing their duties well if they are lethargical or keep on sitting at one place as in that way they would not be able to catch all criminals. The spies themselves should be above board and should not unnecessarily harass anyone. They should be able to go deep into the matter to know the truth. (Rig 9-73-7)
6. The spy should be very quick in reaching any place, wherever and whenever needed. They should know the topography of the place completely and accurately. They should specially be posted in trade and community centres so that the bad element is kept under watch. (Rig 9-73-4)

In Vedas, whereas Varuna has been designated as Police Minister, Kutsa is entrusted with the job of Vigilance Department. In this way Police, spies and vigilance are kept under different Ministers. Kutsa too is a god but here he acts as a human being incharge of Vigilance Department. Since the job of Kutsa is of a sensitive nature, Indra etc. rajas have been shown as his protectors so that he is able to discharge his duties fearlessly. The raja eliminates the enemies with the support of Kutsa and protects the public from their clutches. 'Kutsa' word is taken from Sanskrit word 'Kutsa' meaning 'Avksheman' or finding out deficiencies, defaults etc. Being the Minister of Vigilance under the raja, his job is to find out the defaults, wrongs, deficiencies, corrupt practices of the government employees. He is to ensure that each department performs their job for the utmost well-being of the public with full honesty and integrity so that the targets/ aims of the department are fulfilled. At times, the employees donot work with integrity and do not devote the time and energy required in doing certain jobs; they just while away their time sitting idle and doing nothing resulting in less output. Sometimes employees misuse or misappropriate money or mateiral of the government for their personal use or take bribe from the people for getting their job done and involve in some other kinds of corrupt practices as a result of which the income of the exchequer is affected or the output/turnover is not upto the mark and also the image of the country is down-trodden. As a consequence, the welfare of the public is not done as required or the public is not safe and sound and the country's resources fade away. It is in such situations that the men of vigilance department under 'Kutsa' rise to the occasion, catch such corrupt employees after seeing the lacking in production, reduction in revenues etc. and locating the employees responsible for such short comings. He presents such people before the raja with his report. The raja gets the matter investigated and punishes the guilty. Here it is to be noted that even after the corrupt government servants are caught by the vigilance department, the raja punishes them after satisfying himself by an independent enquiry so that full justice is done in the matter. It is said that being the head of the vigilance department, 'Kutsa' keeps a watch on the corrupt employees as also the employees of his department itself so that they may not, with the collusion of such corrupt employees, involve themselves in such evil practices.

'Kutsa' is the minister of the present day vigilance department. 'Kutsa' word has been taken from 'Kriti' meaning to cut i.e. one who can cut is Kutsa. Kutsa accordingly cuts the corrupt practices or lethargical activities of the staff so this is apt word for this department. 'Kutsa' has been called by several names in vedas:

1. 'Kutsa' is called 'Susarvas' meaning Kutsa is well-versed in various kinds of sciences. He should be of good moral character so that he gets appreciation from all quarters.
2. Kutsa is called 'Annawala'. This is because the men of Kutsa keep a watch on the people responsible for production and distribution of agricultural products. If they are not alert then foodgrains production would go down and the supplies would be deficient to the consumers.

3. Kutsa is called 'Turvayan' meaning that wherever Kutsa or his men go, the employees leave corrupt practices and work as per their dharma and in this way the public at large is benefitted.

4. Kutsa is called 'Atithigava' meaning that Kutsa and his men work as guests for public at large and help them in detecting the evil-doers or corrupt men.

5. Kutsa has been called 'Ayu' meaning that Kutsa and his men are hardworking. They get mixed up with people at root level and see that various things are not mixed up (adulterated) by the people and in this way cheating the public.

6. The raja has to provide proper protection to Kutsa and his men so that after having been adequately paid and properly protected, they discharge their duty fearlessly and vigilantly, inspect the products properly and watch their distribution amongst the consumers. This ensures improvement in production and distribution system.

7. Because of the temptation and corrupt practices, the products are at times misappropriated by the men of the government resulting in deficient supply to public and people become poorer. The men of Kutsa, by their constant endeavour, remove the bottlenecks and deficiencies as a result of which there is proper distribution and all consumers feel satisfied.

In vedas, there is mention of proper protection to be provided to Kutsa and his men by the raja. This is in view of the fact that during the discharge of their duty, the men of Kutsa catch hold of the corrupt employees and get them punished. Consequently these people, who are punished, develop enmity with Kutsa's men and try to harm them in one way or the other by filing complaints against them, beating them, when found in isolation etc. resulting in the Kutsa's men facing difficulty in the discharge of their duties. So, in such a situation the raja has to protect Kutsa and his men. Even today vigilance department is not in a position to discharge their duty properly due to political interference or other pressures. This department, therefore, deserves to be adequately protected. Rig veda says:

प्रान्यच्चकम धृहः सूर्यस्य कुस्तायान्यद् वरिवो यातवेड़कः,
अनासौ दस्यूँरमृणो वधेन निदुर्योण आर्वृगमृध्र वाचः।

Meaning that the raja annihilates the corrupt and adharmic people and for his assistance, posts Kutsa and his men in that department so that it is thereafter run as per tenets of dharma. In this way, Kutsa and his men arrest the corrupt and idle persons and get them punished by the raja after proper investigation about their bad practices. These criminals are given exemplary punishment so that they may not dare repeat the crime and it may prove to be deterrent for others. After the punishment to such persons, the raja assures safety to Kutsa and his men for having detected the guilty persons.

The raja should always be prepared to punish the guilty persons detected by Kutsa and his men. At some places raja and Kutsa have been used in vedas as synonyms. It may be because the jobs of both are same so far as punishment to the guilty is concerned as the raja decides the punishment to be awarded in consultation with Kutsa as Kutsa knows the guilt of the guilty persons better since he had detected such persons found guilty. At times Kutsa and his men also get involved in corrupt practices. Such persons harass the honest persons with a view to extract something out of them by finding faults in such persons and by showering threats on them. In such a situation, the honest persons should have direct access to the raja to file complaint against such persons of Kutsa with a view to save themselves from the clutches of the bribe-seekers. The raja, on receipt of such complaints against Kutsa and his men, orders an independent enquiry and severe punishment is awarded in case Kutsa and his men are found guilty as per complaint.

There is mention about the autonomy granted to Kutsa in the working of his vigilance department in some mantras but it is not possible to narrate here the contents of all these mantras. It is, however, evident that like the present day vigilance department, there is provision of vigilance department working directly under the raja to detect the corrupt employees in the various government departments and get them punished by the raja. Simultaneously the people keep a watch on the conduct of Kutsa and his men also and on finding them guilty, they are more severely punished. In this way everyone thinks that he is being watched upon and is afraid of entering into corrupt practices.

According to vedas, Soma works as the minister for justice under the raja. He has courts under him to try the criminals and award punishment, when found guilty. But such punishment is awarded after proper investigation in the matter and after finding out the truth. Such is the system even today. The Police Vigilance Department detects the criminals and hand them over to judiciary for trial and punishment. So our system in ancient time was like the present system stated to be the innovation of the English. In fact English only saw the Laws of Islam prevailing in Indian courts on their advent to this country and introduction of English system was considered as an improvement over that system instead of resorting to what is contained in our vedas and samritis:

सुविज्ञानं चिकितुषे जनाय सच्चासच्च वचसी पस्पृधाते,
तयोर्यत् सत्यं यतरदूजी यस्तादित् सोमो वतिप्रहन्त्यासत्।।

Meaning that criminals and non-criminals come to courts with their arguments and after finding out the truth, the court acquits and helps the non-criminals and punishes those found criminals. Soma having been shown as Minister for Judiciary, there is a clear provision in vedas about the establishment of judicial courts in ancient India. During trial too the defence was projected like the present day procedure. Also various kinds of crimes committed by such criminals are narrated and punishment is prescribed for each of such crimes commensurate with the magnitude of crime committed and proved. It also shows that in vedas and samritis some provision like the present day provision in Indian Penal Code and Criminal Procedure Code, Civil Procedure Code, Evidence Act are available although while introducing the above codes, English had stated that no proper code for the guidance of the courts was available in India. There is mention of the cases of rape and punishment for the same; as also the cases of people revolting against the government and punishment of death in such cases has been prescribed. It is also mentioned in vedas that in vedic country, persons having difference of opinion in peaceful environ are not to be punished. This is like the 'Freedom of Expression' in present time. Like this, there are so many other cases mentioned in vedas, which have been described as punishable or non-punishable keeping democratic system of governance in view.

आ जिह्वया मूरदेवान् रभस्व (अथ० 8-3-2)

Meaning that persons doing wrong actions out of foolishness are at first warned only and are punished only on repeating the crime. Might be the consideration that the first crime would be out of ignorance and the culprit might be careful in future but recurrence of such crime proves its being intentional. Such criminals are then punished and if still repeated third time, then death punishment is given:

त्रियार्तुधानः प्रसिति त एतु।

Meaning that the culprits are given two chances to improve their behaviour and are punished if they still donot behave. Further, in vedas, Brahmins have been recommended to be appointed as judges—

ब्राह्मण...........स सोमं प्रथमः पपो। (अथ० 4-6-1)

As already indicated, as per vedas, varna is not determined according to birth but it is opted by each individual as per his capability. Therefore, a Brahmin is considered to be well educated person and, therefore, a well-educated person can be the fittest man to become a judge. Further, since the Brahmins are not over-ambitious, they decide the cases without any bias and impartially. Also the Brahmin, can go deep into the case to find out the truth in view of his being well-educated. Still if the Brahmin is not able to impart justice, then appeal lies before the raja and the decision by the raja is acceptable to all ungrudgingly.

3 RAMAYANA PERIOD

As already indicated, Police and CBI are mainly to maintain law and order in the country and its protection from foreign aggression. We have already considered that these organisations did exist, more or less in the present form, in vedic period as per canons of vedas and samritis. These departments, even under the raja, who was responsible for protection of life and property of the subjects from internal criminals and forcign invaders with the help of Police, spies and army and to defray their expenses, used to take a part of the produce as 'Rajbhag'. Such spying system even existed in the realm of gods. Narad is stated to be one such spy, who used to wander about in all lokas and gave information about the universe to the gods and about gods to the rajas of this universe. The information given by Narad was always considered to be reliable and was generally for the well-being of the people and gods. Indra had his own system of gathering secrets of what had been happening in the universe. That is how he came to know, whenever any rishi excelled in tapasya as he always thought that he being the raja of Swarga, such tapasya would be to dislodge him from Swarga. He then used to take appropriate action to save himself either by developing fighting with him or by causing disturbance in his tapsya, by deputing 'Apsaras'. In this way even apsaras were a sort of spies of Indra.

We do not have much literature about the Satya-yug except that of Harish Chandra, whose truthfulness had been tested by Vishwamitra by deputing his spies to check up his way of living and then causing further distress so that he could be persuaded to leave the path of truthfulness. This continued till Harish Chandra was able to establish that he would not leave that path.

The system of spies' organisation continued in Rama rajya in accordance with the provision of vedic tenets. 'Ramcharitmanas' is full of such instances. It starts from the incident when Sati went to her father inspite of Shiva having not agreed to her going there as they had not been invited by Daksha (Sati's father) for the yagya being performed by him and it was not advisable to go uninvited. Sati, however, did go there but since Shiva expected some untoward incident taking place there, he had sent a few of his spies to keep a watch on what happened there. Those spies did create disturbance in the yagya, when Sati gave up her life in view of Daksha having insulted Shiva, and narrated the entire happenings to Shiva on return. Subsequently when Sati became Parvati in next birth, then Narad advised her to perform Tapsya to have Shiva as her husband. Shiva had sent Saptarishi to test her bonafides in her having undertaken to marry Shiva only. They tested Parvati and then reported back to Shiva about her strong intention of having Shiva as her husband. Shiva himself had come incognito as a Brahmin at the time of Ram's birth to have his 'Darshan'. In the darbar of Dasratha, full team of spies was on work, which continued during the entire period of Ram rajya too.

When Ram and Lakshman went to Janakpuri along with Vishwamitra at the time of Sita's swayamber, then Janak's spies were at work and they immediately advised Janak of Vishwamitra's arrival and then Janak came to officially receive him. Similarly all happenings in marriage could be known by Janak through his spies. Even Parsuram must be in touch with some spies because of which he could know the Shiva dhanush having been broken and immediately he reached at the swayamber.

Subsequently, when Ram was to be coronated, the gods came to know of it. It shows that they were keeping constant touch with the happenings in Oudh and immediately gods went to Saraswati to help them so that Ram is not coronated and he goes to forests to kill the rakshasas. Saraswati too through her spies, coached Manthra about Ram's coronation and its effects on Kaikayee. Manthra then briefed Kaikayee about it and it culminated in Ram having to go to forests and the coronation of Bharat. Possibly the queens too had their system of knowing what was happening in the rajya and Manthra would be one such spy, who collected information about Ram's coronation and then briefed Kaikayee of the same. Next day when Raja Dasratha did not come out of mahal, the public sent Sumant to check up the matter. Sumant only had the access to mahal as a person allowed to go to mahal had to be of confidence of raja and then there would have been a system as to which matter of Rajmahal should be known to others and which should not be known by all but a few ones only. Even to Sumant, Kaikayee did not tell about what had happened and asked him to send Ram, who only could know it from Dasratha. When Ram came there only then Kaikayee told entire thing. Subsequently when Ram prepared to go to forests, Sita and Lakshman could know this fact from their people and they also went with Ram to forests. Oudh people accompanied Ram to forests, but since Ram did not want it, he woke up in the night and proceeded further eliminating the signs of the wheels of chariot so that the people could not know where they had gone. These were all ways of keeping things secret. In the forests also the rishis had their people all around, who kept the rishis apprised of what had been happening in the surroundings. Balmik could know of Ram's arrival in advance. Similarly Bhardwaj could know it too through their men acting as spies.

On Rama and Lakshman having gone to forests, Bharat had gone to meet them in forests. Nishadraj's spies told him of Bharat going with army and sensing some bad designs, he prepared to fight with Bharat. Situation, however, could be handled after knowing Bharat's intentions. Similarly Lakshman too got ready to give a fight to Bharat taking him coming with bad intention and then 'akashvani' saved the situation. In those days even 'Devvani' or 'akashwani' could tell the things to happen and generally saved a bad situation.

On Rama, Sita and Lakshman having gone to forests and Dasratha having died, Raja Janak had been keeping a watch on what had been happening in Oudh. He was, however, not able to go to Oudh, on arrival of Bharat there as Ram and Bharat, both were his sons-in-law and he could not decide whether to favour Ram or welcome Bharat's coronation, ignoring what happened to Ram. To save himself from such a situation, he did not visit Oudh. It was only after he came to know that Bharat was not anxious to have rajya and had gone to forests to meet Ram to be Oudh's Raja, that Raja Janak too went to forests to meet them there. Raja Janak had also told this fact when he went to forests to clear his position of long silence in the matter. When in forests too the job of who should be Oudh's raja came up for discussion and Raja Janak very wisely decided to accept Ram as Oudh's Raja and Bharat to work as his lieutenant for 14 years, after which, Bharat would hand over the rajya to the real successor i.e. Ram. In this way Janak saved the situation — one whom to accept raja of Oudh out of Ram and Bharat and another this being the family affair of Oudh, Janak did not consider it advisable to interfere in the affair and at one time, when the question came on him to decide, Janak did say that:

"सिथिल सनेह गुनत मन माहीं,
आए इहां कीन्ह भल नाहीं।

As the matter was rather sensitive, and it was not possible either to make Bharat agree to become raja or convince Ram to go back and become raja of Oudh as he had come on his father's orders and in the absence of father, who had since died, no one else could revoke those orders. Subsequently when the question was solved, Raja Janak came to Oudh along with Bharat and coached him about the system of governance and then only went to Janakpuri.

Ram wanted to annihilate the rakshasas without anyone else interfering in the matter. So he went from Chitrakoot to Panchvati. On the way, many rishis came to know of Ram's arrival in the forests through their men and they all met him. On the other side the rakshasas too were keeping a watch on what was happening in the forests. Sarupnakha could reach Panchvati and seeing Ram and Lakshman there proposed herself to them and on neither agreeing to the same, she threatened them on which, her ears and nose had been cut. She told this to Khar and Doosan, who came to fight with Ram with a big army. Ram defeated them and then Sarupnakha went to Ravana and narrated the whole thing to him. She also told that his spies were not quite active and had become lethargic having lived in all pleasures of Lanka, that is why he had not so far known about Ram and Lakshman having come there; having killed many rakshasas in the forests, including Khar and Doosan. So in this way there had been some lacking on the part of the spies of Ravana. Sarupnakha had said:

करसि पान सोवसि दिनु राती,
सुधि नहिं तव सिर पर आराती।

It will be observed that spying had been the most essential ingredient of governance and without proper spying, the raja would not be able to know what had been happening in the state as also in other neighbouring states, who could any time attack. Even rakshasas had to be vigilant about it as vindicated by Sarupnakha. On knowing about the death of Khar and Doosan, Ravana immediately imagined that they could not be killed by ordinary persons and the tapsavi must be Brahma himself and he should develop enmity with him so that by being killed by him, he could attain salvation. He, therefore, secretly planned to kidnap Sita. He went to Marich, and asked him to become golden deer so that when Ram went for hunting it, he could kidnap Sita in his absence. This all worked and Ram and Lakshman had been wandering about in forests in search of Sita. Sugreeva lived on the mountain. He too had been living there hiding himself from his brother Bali. He, therefore, had kept his spies all around to keep him apprised of any planning by Bali against him. These spies advised of Ram and Lakshman coming towards that hill. With a view to know their whereabouts, Sugreeva sent Hanuman incognito to find out who they were and advise him by a signal, so that he could run away from that place. Hanuman brought Ram and Lakshman to Sugreeva after having been assured of their bonafides. Ram sent Sugreeva to challenge Bali. At that time Bali's wife Tara had already known through her spies that Sugreeva had come on inspiration from Ram, who had come from Oudh and so she checked Bali from entering into a battle with Sugreeva, but Bali did fight and was killed by Ram.

Subsequently to find out Sita, Sugreeva sent vanaras in all directions (obviously to work secretly) and to intimate her whereabouts within a month's time. The spies had to be assigned time-bound jobs and in case of failure to do the job, they had to lose their lives as well. Therefore, the spies had to be very alert and confident of carrying out the assigned jobs. Hanuman went incognito to Lanka, searched Sita in every mahal but could not find her. Then he saw Vibheesana's Ashram. The spies could know whom to approach, whom to disclose their identity and so on. Finding Vibheesana as Rambhakta, he disclosed his identity and purpose of visit. Vibheesana guided him to Ashoka Vatika. Again since Ravana had come there at that time, Hanuman hided himself. So a spy had to know all these tricks. After Ravana had left, he met Sita, assured her of his bonafides by showing the insignia given by Ram. The spies were accordingly entrusted with some insignia by the rajas to be used in case of need. He then started eating fruits in the vatika and had beaten a few of the gardeners, who complained to Ravana. Ravana sent his son, who had also been killed by Hanuman. Then Ravana sent Meghnada with the instructions, not to kill, but to catch him so that his whereabouts could be known. It was, therefore, always advisable to catch the spies in other's country with a view to extract information about his purpose of visit and about his country. Hanuman was caught and produced before Ravana. He spoke very fearlessly in Ravana's darbar so much so that Ravana was annoyed and ordered his being killed but then Vibheesana advised that the representative of a king should not be killed as per rules.

"नीति विरोध न मारिये दूता"

This indicates that there were detailed rules about ambassadorial immunities and how to deal with such people including spies. It was decided to burn his tail and spare his life so that his master could know the correct facts lest the spy should misguide him. Hanuman burnt the entire Lanka and went to Ram after taking some insignia or acknowledgement from Sita to be shown to Ram in confirmation of his having done the job. Hanuman told Ram, how the security arrangements had been made in Lanka, the fortification of the entire area so that Ram could plan attacking Lanka accordingly. In this way the spies had been doing great jobs for the master even staking their lives for such jobs. That is why the spies had direct access to their master rajas. While in Lanka, Hanuman saw:

गिरि पर चढ़ि लंका तेहिं देखी, कहि न जाइ अति दुर्गविशेषी,
अति उतंग जलनिधि चहुपासा, कनक कोट कर परम प्रकासा।

This is how the spies had been entrusted with the jobs of finding out everything about the enemy's place. Hanuman checked up this all by climbing on a hilltop from where he could see Lanka. It was a big fort, surrounded by sea from all sides; then there was a long boundary wall and then the town was adequately protected by rakshasas from all sides so much so that even a mosquito could not enter Lanka, what to speak of human beings. In such a situation, how difficult the job for the spy had been, can be imagined. But Hanuman was capable of doing it all because of his being brave, intelligent, could work incognito and could courageously act in the darbar of Ravana. Hanuman could have gone secretly without having been noticed after having met Sita but then his job was also to demoralise Ravana by showing his strength as also to find out all about his darbar etc. So Hanuman decided to get himself arrested and face the consequences. His burning Lanka had the desired effect of having demoralised all in Lanka so much so that even Ravana was all in praise for him even before Angad when he went to meet Ravana. Hanuman's job was also to apprise Ravana of Ram's strength so that he could beg to be excused by Ram, returning Sita to him.

After Hanuman's return and having known the

whereabouts of Sita, Ram proceeded to Lanka with his army. Now Ravana's spies net-work was at job and every bit of information was being conveyed to Ravana and Ravana in turn had been constantly consulting his advisors. He had known when Ram had come on the other side of the sea and it was at that time during consultation with his advisers that Vibheesana had been expelled from Lanka on his having advised Ravana for returning Sita and submitting before Ram. Vibheesana had joined Ram. Now on Vibheesana having sought refuge under Ram, Ram consulted his people, who generally were not in favour of his affording refuge as he would convey all Ram's secrets to Ravana, the enemy. This is what is fair policy too but then Ram was confident of his victory as also he, as a matter of principle, could not refuse affording refuge to the incumbent. Ram told all this to Sugreeva and granted refuge to Vibheesana as Ram thought that in case he really wished to join Ram, then he would be helpful in telling about Lanka and subsequent preparations for the battle in Lanka etc. So the strategic policy also speaks about winning over the men of the enemy. This is what British had been doing in India in fighting with the local rajas/nawabs. By purchasing the Commander Mir Jafar, British defeated Siraj-ud-daula. By winning Sikh commanders, they defeated Sikhs, when they were at winning point. By creating division in various rajas and putting them one against another, they could rule over the entire India. So it was not in fact correct for Ravana to have expelled Vibheesana at that time and having allowed him to join Ram as had been pronounced by Vibheesana in Ravana's darbar itself. Ravana had, however, sent his spies following Vibheesana's expulsion with a view to know what happened to him after meeting Ram. The spies had given full report of Vibheesana having been granted refuge. Then Ravana thought of creating similar division in Ram's men and sent his spies to win over Sugreeva. But Sugreeva did not yield. His faithfulness had been appreciated by Ram. Rakshasas were very capable spies as they could change their forms, could become animals, birds etc and without the enemy knowing their presence, they could know everything about the enemy. One great advantage of Vibheesana having joined Ram was that he could recognise all such rakshasas coming incognito as he knew all their arts. Since the spy's job is to tell all sorts of bad or good news about the enemy, some information was not digestible to Ravana, when it amounted to appreciation of Ram and in such a situation, the spies had to face thrashing from Ravana.

When Ram crossed the sea and reached Lanka, Ravana could know it. He consulted his advisers about the future course of action. On the other side, Ram had sent Angad, as his ambassador to Ravana to once again persuade him if he could surrender before Ram. This shows how much peace-loving the Indians had been and resorted to war only after all efforts of negotiating peace had proved non-fruitful. On Ravana not having agreed to surrender, battle started. Vibhccsana had advised about who to be posted with how many people on all gates of entry to Lanka. The army was divided accordingly and then attacked. As Ram was the aggressor here, the attack had to be from him only. There were spies and spies on both sides — Vibheesana's men in Lanka and Ravana's men in Ram's army. Vibheesana's spies kept him informed about what had been happening in Lanka. Vibheesana alerted Ram, when Kumbhkarna had been awakened and he came for fighting; he told Ram when Meghnada had been performing an important yagya, which could give him enormous power to fight and subsequently when Ravana too had been conducting such yagya, and ultimately it is Vibheesana, who told Ram, after Ram was not able to kill Ravana and all his heads and arms could crop up a new after having been cut by Ram, that Ravana could be killed after an 'Amrit Kund' in his abdomen was dried up by an 'Agniban'. In fact Ram had been waiting Vibheesana to tell so as he wanted to test the bonafides and affinity of Vibheesana with him or with his brother Ravana. Ravana was accordingly killed. This led to the saying :

"घर का भेदी लंका ढावे"

In this way, spies were mainly responsible for telling all about the enemy after which only the war strategy was drawn, and consequent victory in the battle. During the war,

Ravana's intelligence department was also alert. The news of Lakshman having become unconscious reached Ravana immediately. He could also know of the Vaid Sukhen having been taken by Hanuman and the vaid having told about bringing 'Sanjeevani booty' from Himalayas. That is how Ravana engaged Kalnemi, a rakshas, to create obstacles in Hanuman's way so that he was not able to reach back by next morning by which time Sanjeevani was to be brought to be of any use. Hanuman had initially come in his trap but subsequently he came to know of his actual position and killed him. Ravana too could know of Kalnemi having been killed. He immediately burnt all plants in Himalayas so that Hanuman was not able to recognise the 'booty'. Hanuman then picked up the entire hillock. When he was passing through Oudh, Bharat's men told about him to Bharat. So Bharat's spies were also at work. Bharat made him fall down. Hanuman narrated all that had happened and then came to Ram. In this way, Ravana had been creating one obstacle after another for Hanuman but ultimately Hanuman could cross all hurdles. Lakshman could thus be cured.

As already indicated, gods had their hand in Ram going to forests and killing the rakshasas. They had been watching Ram-Ravana battle with keenness.

Ram having been on foot and Ravana on chariot, Indra sent his chariot and sarthy for Ram's use. Subsequently when Ram, Lakshman had been tied in 'Nagpasha', Narada sent Garuda to release them from the nagpasha. After Ravana had been killed, all gods came to praise Ram. Ram then asked Indra to enliven the vanaras, who gave their lives for the cause of gods. During Ram-Ravana battle, full war strategy has been displayed e.g. who should fight with whom and when and with how many soldiers and with which arm, has aptly, been displayed in this battle, along with the job of spies at every stage.

On return from Lanka, Ram, Lakshman and Sita did not straightaway go to Ayodhaya but at first Hanuman was sent incognito to find out the intention of Bharat as to whether he still had been waiting for Ram to come and if he had adjusted to governance then he would better not go there. It may also be possible as Bharat had himself been thinking, that since Bharat did not care to either help Ram or to know about his well-being even after Hanuman had apprised him of Ram-Ravana war, Ram's coming over to Ayodhaya may not be desirable. Be as it may, when Hanuman came to Ayodhaya as a Brahmin and he found Bharat anxiously waiting for Ram's arrival. Hanuman went back and gave report to Ram after which only he came to Ayodhaya.

Ram was coronated in Ayodhaya. He was well-versed with the canons of governance. He knew that for the raja, the top duty was to protect the subjects from internal crimes; external aggressions; make all essential commodities available at reasonable rates and in full measurement. He ensured all this. This could again be possible with a well-knit spies' net, strong army and able policemen. So it has to be assumed that all these were available in Ram rajya to make it an ideal rajya. Ram's spies had direct access to him and were free to tell all sorts of happenings — good or bad — so much so that on having known from a washerman rebuking his wife for having stayed away during the night that he was not Ram, who could keep Sita even after her stay in Lanka for a long period, Ram separated Sita. Ram himself too used to go to the town during the nights incognito to have the first hand information about what had been happening in the kingdom. Such a practice even kept the spies and king's men alert. It shows that in Ram rajya:

1. There was well knit net-work of spies.
2. The spies had free access to the raja.
3. The spies could meet the raja in seclusion any time — day or night.
4. The spies did their jobs secretly and public could not make out their presence anywhere.
5. The public could freely criticise the raja and his way of governance meaning thereby that there was freedom of expression by public.

6. The spies had to make raja aware of whatever they could know — good or bad.
7. The raja had to satisfy the public on any objectionable issue. Ram did enquire into the question of Sita's bonafides as alleged by the washerman and after having known that this was quite amply prevalent in public, he separated Sita after consulting his Sabha.
8. The appointment of spies was out of specially expert people, who could change their form and wander about incognito. They were also fully aware of the topography of the place of posting.
9. The well-being of the subjects was the primary duty of the raja. That is why at the time of going to forests, he had told Lakshman, when he insisted to accompany him:

जासु राज प्रिय प्रजा दुखारी, सो नृप अवसि नरक अधिकारी।

10. To keep the praja pleased, the raja had to know the position by having tours incognito, to see that his men had not been harassing the public and no evil activities were in existence in public. Such nuisances, wherever and whenever detected, were immediately redressed.
11. In Ram rajya —

बयरु न कर काहू सन कोई, राम प्रताप विषमता खोई।
and "दंड जतिन्ह कर भेद जहँ"।

There was no enmity among the individuals against anyone and since all had been acting according to law and religion, there was no crime and consequently no punishment. It is said that in those days the word 'dand' was used not for awarding punishment but the stick kept by the Sanyasis. Since there was no crime and everyone was living as per his religion, all people were happy —

हरषित रहहिं नगर के लोगा,
करहिं सकल सुर दुर्लभ भोगा।

12. So far as the protection from external aggression is concerned, Ram had all rajas under him as his vassals. This had been confirmed in the Aswamedha yagyas held by him from time to time in which all vassal states used to acknowledge the suzerainty of the Raja of Oudh.

13. All were living as per religion or the tenets of vedas and smritis so much so that Bali, a vassal raja under Oudh, had been killed by Ram as he had misbehaved with his brother Sugreeva in having expelled him from the kingdom and having snatched his wife as well. Ram himself had said:

अनुज वधू भगिनी सुत नारी, सुनु सठ कन्या सम ए चारी,
इन्हहिं कुदृष्टि बिलोकई जोई, ताहिं वधें कछु पाप न होई।

Such was the morality amongst the people and anyone who violated such morality was punished by death. Kiskindhya being a vassal state of Oudh, it was the duty of Ram, as Raja of Oudh or Bharat's representative there to punish Bali, who had misbehaved with Sugreeva. Even then Ram coronated Angad, Bali's son, as the 'Yuvraj' (successor) since as Bali's son, he was the valid successor to throne after Bali's death. It was a system in those days that even when a raja defeated another, the rajya of the defeated raja was handed over to his successor to be ruled as an autonomous ruler after payment of some war-damages (compensation) and accepting the suzerainty of the winning raja. Similarly after killing Ravana, Vibheesana was made the ruler of Lanka. This is also confirmed by Ram, when after his coronation in Oudh, he had bade 'good bye' to the rajas, Sugreeva, Vibheesana. who accompanied him to Oudh saying :

अब गृह जाहु सखा सब भजेहु मोहि दृढ़ नेम,
सदा सर्वगत सर्वहित जानि करेहु अति प्रेम।

Here Ram had reminded them of their being his vassals, and advised them to govern keeping the well-being of the subjects in view.

14. All were happy in Ram rajya is clear from the following.

राम राज नभगेस सुनु सचराचर जग माहिं,
काल कर्म सुभाव गुन कृत दुख काहुहि नाहिं।

15. The raja, apart from his normal duty of protecting the subjects from internal crime and external aggression and keeping them happy, considered themselves duty-bound to care for their ultimate salvation too. Such is not the position today. In this connection, Ram had once invited all in a conference and told about the 'bhakti` as the means of attaining salvation but since this was not to be enforced by the raja, it was left to the people to abide by his advice or not. Ram said:

सुनहु सकल पुरजन मम बानी, कहउं न कछु ममता उर आनी।
नहिं अनीति नहिं कछु प्रभुताई, सुनहु करहु जो तुम्हहिं सोहाई।

In this way the raja cared for the public's ultimate salvation. The praja was quite happy in such a rajya and they were always prepared to give up their lives for the sake of the rajya. It is only in subsequent period of Rajputs when public did not associate themselves with the raja in the protection of the kingdom from foreign invaders due to the indifferent treatment by the raja that we lost to the foreign invasions by Sungas, Huns, Kushans, Muslims and ultimately British inspite of India's having been very brave, most educated and most advanced people of the universe. So for a better governance, the raja has to consider the subjects like his children and the subjects too should be prepared to give up their lives for the sake of the raja as in Ram rajya.

4 KRISHNA PERIOD

We have already seen how as per vedic tenets, the Police and CBI jobs were done by the spies and the raja in Ram rajya. Raja's men had been posted at every nook and corner of the kingdom to locate if there was any person indulging in undesirable activities. They would catch such people and present before the 'raja' for suitable punishment. Raja himself had also been touring the kingdom incognito to see if his men had been doing their job alright.

We do not have sufficient documented literature on what has happened in different ages. Of course about incarnations and their conduct, we get material from Hindu's epics. Such material for Ram period is available in Ramcharitmanas, Balmiki Ramayan. After Ram, we come to Krishna period. Material about Krishna period is available in Srimad Bhagwat. In Srimad Bhagwat, apart from Krishna, we get some material about all other incarnations and the rajas of Pauranic period. Since the raja was expected to primarily protect the people from internal criminals and foreign aggression, the raja was generally elected by the people as may be capable of doing this job. Alternatively, the raja used to nominate his successor and get him approved by his Sabha too. Since the Sabha comprised of the representatives of the people, the raja was considered to have the consent of the people. Raja Dasratha had wanted Ram to be his successor. For this purpose, he at first obtained the approval of Guru Vasistha and then of the Sabha. Generally the theory of primogenitor i.e. the eldest son becoming the successor was followed but this could be changed if the eldest son was not considered capable of becoming a raja. In case where only one son was available, he was made raja because the kingdom could not be kept without a raja even for a single day. But in such cases, the conduct of the raja had to be seen and if he was not found upto the mark, then he could be dethroned too. This is what had happened in the case of Raja Bain. Being the only son, he was crowned and on his not conducting well, he had been warned too but on his still not mending his ways, he had been killed by the Sabha and another person Prithu, who was still young, was made the raja. Raja Prithu was :

1. A very strong raja. He had a strong army too and by dint of a strong army, he had conquered large areas and added to his kingdom.
2. Although he had been caring about the well-being of the people and had been checking the same through his spies, he was generally upset :

अनतर्बहिश्च भूतानां पश्यन् कर्माणि चारणै,
उदासीन इवाध्यक्ष्ये वायुरात्मेव देहिनाम । (भागवत)

3. He was so much a follower of religion that inspite of the punishable enemy's son, he pardoned him and did not pardon his own son, when found punishable.
4. He was the ruler of the entire universe and all in his kingdom were happy.
5. He respected all people and honoured brahmins and rishis etc.
6. He treated the praja as his children and the praja too cared for the raja more than their ownselves.
7. He loved the sanyasis and munis and was very strict towards the criminals in punishing them.

Such a capable raja ruled the entire universe. He used to tour his kingdom with dhanushban in his hand so that the culprit, if any found, could be punished then and there. He ruled the kingdom with the help of the team of spies, who used to report even minutest matters for his consideration.

Similarly, Harinakshyap having been cruel to his people,

had been killed by Narsingha Bhagwan and Prahlad succeeded him. In this way, in case of a raja being cruel and not caring for his people, he was dethroned by the people or killed by God incarnation. During Kansa's period, at the time of the marriage of Devki and Vasudeva, there was an 'Akashwani' indicating that Devki's eighth child would kill him. In this way the 'akashwanis' were generally to alert the people from ensuing bad happenings or telling about good things to come or checking from a wrong action. Akashwanis were, therefore, a way of checking crime like the Police. There was adequate spies' net in Kansa's rajya and he could know the birth of Krishna in Gokul and sent many of his spy rakshasas to kill him. These spy rakshasas went there incognito and attacked Krishna. He, however, escaped from all such attacks. Kansa was keeping Akroor in his kingdom although he was a Yadav. Akroor too was staying there with a view to safeguard the interests of Yadavas in the kingdom, when all other Yadavas had left the kingdom and gone to some other countries. Kansa used Akroor in bringing Krishna and Balram with the planning to kill them, thinking that they would come in view of their having confidence in Akroor and this happened too. But Krishna demolished all Kansa's designs and killed the brave rakshasas retained by Kansa for killing Krishna and Balram and subsequently killed Kansa too. Kansa, however, did not attack on Nanda as rakshas rajas too had their principles and Nand would have been under Kansa's suzerainty guaranteeing him protection so far as he continued to pay annual tribute. There is mention of Nanda having gone to Mathura to deliver goods to Kansa in lieu of annual contribution. After killing Kansa, Raja Ugarsen (Kansa's father) was crowned.

There were similar many Asura rajas at that time and they all had their net-work of spies, who used to give them information about what had been happening in their respective kingdoms and in the kingdoms of other rajas or the designs of other rajas on their kingdoms. Jarasandha had been attacking Dwarka after finding out through his spies that Krishna was out. Krishna used to get all information through his spies. Leaving aside the rajas, even gods had kept their spies in

India. When Krishna forbade Nanda from worshipping Indra and instead worshipping their Goverdhana and cows, Indra came to know of it and harassed the Brijwasis by heavy rains and storms. Krishna, however, saved them by bringing all under Goverdhana and Indra, accepting defeat begged to be excused. Narada too had once come to Dwarka with a view to know Krishna's behaviour with his so many queens and went satisfied having seen equal behaviour with all. So Narada, as usual, had been acting as a spy between gods and rajas of India and vice-versa as also between the rajas themselves and he was relied upon by everyone. There is mention of spies during Krishna period at various other places too such as :

1. Krishna after killing Kansa had sent Udhava as his spy to check up the position of the Brijwasis in his absence. He resembled Krishna but the gopies recognised him and impressed him by their love for Krishna.
2. Krishna sent Akroor as his representative/ spy to check up the behaviour of Dhritrastra towards Pandvas. He apprised Krishna of the correct position.
3. Krishna had known through his intelligence the attempt to kill Pandvas in Lakshagriha and saved them.
4. At the time of Rukmani's marriage, Rukmani had sent a spy Brahmin to Krishna to apprise him of her love for him but his brother and father wanted to marry her with Shishupal. Krishna immediately left for Rukmani's place and kidnapped her by a secret plan and then married with her.
5. After having saved themselves from Lakshagriha, Pandvas lived in forests incognito and they had been getting information about all that had been happening in Hastinapur and in other parts of the country through their spies. That is how they reached Panchal at the time of Daropadi's swayamber and married with Daropadi.

   It is here that Kaurvas came to know of the Pandvas escape from Lakshagriha.
6. After Daropadi's chirharan, Pandvas had to live in forests

for 13 years of which for one year they had to live in hiding. If they could be located during that one year, they would have to repeat the period of exile. But inspite of the best efforts of Kaurvas to locate them by sending their spies in every nook and corner, they could not trace them. They could be found only after the period of exile was over.

7. Arjun went incognito to Dwarka as a Dandi Sadhu and met Subhadra (Krishna's sister) and subsequently married with her. Even Balram could not recognise him during that period. This had to be done as Balram wanted Subhadra to be married with Duryodhan and Krishna wanted her marriage with Arjun. So this planning.

8. Sudama came to Krishna for help but he could not ask for it. Krishna, however, had known everything through his spies and provided everything at his residence, which even Sudama could know after reaching there.

9. Bhagwan went to Bali as Baman incognito but Shukracharya, the Guru of Bali, had recognised him and had warned Bali against agreeing to accede to his request. But Bali fulfilled his promise of granting three steps land.

10. In Krishna Lila, all gods, goddesses, included Shiva, used to come incognito and enjoyed the same.

11. Kansa had sent many rakshasas incognito to kill Krishna in Brij.

12. At his birth itself Krishna had been taken by Vasudeva secretly to Brij from the prison and no one could know the secret unless at later stage Narada told Kansa about it.

13. Aswatthama had secretly killed five sons of Daropadi, when they were asleep taking them as five Pandvas.

14. During Mahabharata, so many times the secrets of the parties were checked up through spies by each of Kauravas and Pandvas so much so that the fact that Karna was Kunti's son, could be known at later time only. This fact had been kept secret by Kunti.

Krishna had come as incarnation of God to kill the asuras. At that time, there were many asura rajas having their spies in all the countries. They had been fighting with each other and could know of the extent of preparation by the enemy through their spies only. Even Kansa had called Krishna to Mathura secretly and had planned to get him killed in Mathura through rakshasas. Whenever Krishna went out of Dwarka, one or the other asura raja used to attack Dwarka. Krishna too could know through his spies of such attacks and he used to reach to face the asura raja in time. Jarasandha had attacked Dwarka 17 times and every time without any prior notice.

Even Dwarka had been constructed in the sea as a fort and it was not easy for anyone to enter Dwarka.

Protection of public was the primary duty of the raja and all lived safe and secure in Dwarka. Krishna's sons and grandsons, who were equal in bravery to Krishna, were able to face the aggressors. They used to bring a lot of wealth to Dwarka after defeating various asura rajas. The rains were in time in Dwarka, foodgrain production was adequate and there were heaps of gold, jewels. so much so that in case of untimely death of any ward, king was held responsible, taking that there would have been some deficiency in the king pleasing the gods. Once a Brahmin's son died. The Brahmin placed the dead body at raja's gate saying that he was responsible for such death. Subsequently nine sons of Brahmin died in young age and the Brahmin used to place each one at Krishna's mahal's gate. Once Arjun had come there and he assured to save the son next time but still same thing happened. Then Krishna and Arjun brought all the sons of the Brahmin from Yamloka and handed over to the Brahmin; meaning thereby that the duties of the raja were multifarious in those days. Apart from Jarasandha, so many other asura rajas attacked Dwarka and Krishna killed them all, culminating in Mahabharata. Krishna's purpose of incarnation was to annihilate all rakshasas. He achieved this object with the help of his lacs of sons and grandsons but subsequently Krishna saw his sons and grandsons too had become very leisurely and nuisance to the people. So he, through some Brahmin's curse passed on them, managed their annihilation too by their fighting with each other. This is how for the sake of peace in public, the raja could even sacrifice his offspring if it was not behaving properly. In Mahabharata, as already indicated, the spies of each party had been collecting information about the preparedness of the other party and passed on to their masters. Dharitrastra sitting in Hastinapur also used to get entire information about the battle. Aswamedha yagyas were held with a view to see that the vassal states recognised the Chakravarty Raja as their suzerain ruler. Yudhisthra had held several such yagyas.

In Bhagwat, there is also mention of the battle between Krishna and Bhomasura showing how Bhomasura had fortified his town for the protection of his subjects from foreign aggressions. His capital was Pragjyotishpur. It was difficult for anyone to enter that town. At first the mountains were there on all sides. Then there was trench all around; then there was a wall with electric current passing through it showing that electricity too was there in those days; then there was vacuum created and filled with poisonous gas; then were the strong nets on all sides and then the brave fighters—

गिरि दुर्गैः शस्त्रदुर्गैर्जलाग्न्यनिलदुर्गमम,
मुरपाशार्युतघोरे दृढ़ैः सर्वत आवृतम। (भागवत)

Such fortification shows the technological marvel of India in those days.

5 MAURYA PERIOD TO RAJPUT PERIOD

We do not have much literature after Mahabharata. It seems there were many small states between Kabul to Gangetic Plains and there were mostly dynastical rulers, who protected their own kingdoms from foreign aggression and cared for the well-being of their people. There was nothing like India in their view. There is some mention of the later states like those of Avanti, Gandhara, Kausal, Magadha, Panchal etc. They had been fighting with each other and so had to keep armed forces for facing such aggressions and their own armed men for maintaining internal peace. These states were quite rich, which tempted foreigners too to invade. These included Greeks under Alexander, Sungas, Kushans, Huns and Muslims culminating in the advent of British. These invasions were mostly from North West and the sufferers were Sind, Panjab, Afghanistan (which was India's part then) and Kashmir. There was no unity amongst these kings to fight jointly against the foreign aggressor rather they tried to help such invaders out of their inter-states rivalries and jealousies. Raja Ambi of Taxila had similarly helped Alexander in his fight against Porus as he considered Porus as his enemy. Alexander invaded in 327 B.C. through Hindukush. He got help from Raja Ambi. He saw huge army of Raja Porus on the other side of Jhelum. He was afraid of facing such a huge army. So he left a part of his army at one place and went upstream with the remaining. He crossed Jhelum during night and suddenly attacked on Porus's force, who were taken unawares. Raja Porus had kept elephants in the front, then horseman, then chariots and then troops on foot. Alexander attacked with bows and arrows and injured the elephants, who rather than crushing enemy's army went back and crushed Porus's army instead, and thus Porus was defeated. This shows that:

1. There was lack of spies with Porus so much so that Alexander changed the place of crossing Jhelum and Porus could not know it.
2. Alexander had made himself fully aware of the topography of that area with the help of Raja Ambi. It helped him in drawing war strategy.
3. Alexander had calculated that he could win over Porus only by sudden attack and he acted accordingly.
4. Alexander mostly used bows and arrows, which infuriated elephants, who crushed Porus's army. Further with bows and arrows, one could attack from a distant place whereas with sword or spears, used by Porus, it could only be close fighting.
5. Battle strategy of Porus was poor. He kept elephants in the front, who, when injured, crushed his army.
6. Whereas Alexander, who was alien, had checked up entire topography of the area, Porus did not care to even know the type of land near the battle field. It was all mud and his army could not fight in muddy land and his chariots and army on foot got entrapped in the mud.

In this way Raja Porus was defeated and Alexander became the first foreign ruler on Indian land. Some petty rajas surrendered and could not fight with Alexander particularly after he had defeated the strong Raja Porus. Alexander, however, could not proceed further to Ravi river as his army refused to proceed further. Might be he had to face the mighty empire of Magadha thereafter. On return, Alexander was killed but he had established his garrisons in India while going back.

At that time Chandra Gupta Maurya came on the scene. His Prime Minister was Chanakya (Kautilya). His Arthashastra is world known policy on governance. Chandra Gupta became ruler of India with his guidance only. He initially became ruler of Magadha and then extended his kingdom defeating Seleucus, the Greek ruler of North-Western area. In Arthashastra, there is detailed narration of the raja's duties, diplomacy, war strategy, economic management, spies net-work etc. Chanakya had compiled Arthashastra with the help of existing vedas, shastras etc. So these tenets were already there and would have been followed in the past but had faded away in course of time. Chanakya again brought them in a condensed form in his Arthashastra. This had been followed by Indian rulers after Mauryas and perhaps by Muslim rulers and British rulers too.

According to Chanakya, the success of a king mostly depended upon his advisers, ministers etc. Therefore, the ministers had to be properly selected and trained. At the time of their selection, their antecedents, family background and their capability should be checked up. Likewise the antecedents of all governors/commissioners should also be got verified. Their integrity and worth should be got checked up through spies. For this purpose, the raja should appoint lady and gent spies. This also indicates that firstly the ladies were literate during that period and they also worked with men in all fields. Chanakya had stressed on the necessity of the trained, confident and capable spies, who were considered as back-bone of the empire. He has indicated nine kinds of spies as under:

1. Kaptika (कापटिक): These were spies, who lived like the students. They were to look into the interest of the raja and his ministers and if they came to know of anything being cooked up against them, they were obliged to apprise the raja of the same.
2. Udasthita (उदास्थित): These spies lived like sanyasis. They were quite intelligent, simple and pious people. They used to intermingle with the traders and start doing those vocations with the help of Kaptika spies. The earnings from that vocation were used for the living of the sanyasis and the students and they kept a watch on the weights and measurements used and the rates charged for sales by the traders. Any overcharging or underweighing was reported to the king.
3. Grihapatitha (गृहपतिथ): These were intelligent, honest spies living like poor traders. Their job was to perform agriculturists' job in farms and keep a watch on other

agriculturists to see that they gave correct share of their products as raja's share.

4. Vedehaka (वेदेहका): Like Udasthita spies, they too joined the traders and performed the jobs of traders and agriculturists with a view to see that there was no cheating in their vocation.

5. Tapsa (तापस): They lived like Tapasvis and doing intelligence work for the raja. They lived near the towns along with student spies, apparently living on small quantity of foodgrains, but secretly eating whatever they liked, so that the traders would take them as tapasvis/ascetics and honour them by heavy payments of money. They should spread word through the students that they are great yogis, who could tell about future. In this way they used to collect information regarding the wealth, family and resources of the traders. They should tell about some gains in the near future and the fellow spies should then manage for such short gains so that the traders develop confidence in such tapasvis and disclose their all to them. Such information could be passed on to the king, to be used for appropriate action against the traders. They could even tell that shortly they would be meeting some high official, minister and to fulfil such foretelling, they would arrange for such meetings too with a view to develop full confidence in the people to extract any information from them about themselves and others.

6. Satree (सत्री): These were close persons of the raja, well-versed with the jyotish, changing their forms, tellers of good or bad things to take place, knowing mesmerism, good/bad omens, dancing. These spies kept wandering from one place to another and during the process collected requisite information and communicated the same to the raja.

7. Tikshan (तीक्षण): These were the spies who were very brave and without caring for themselves could fight with ferocious animals like lions. They mixed up with brave warriors with a view to know their resources. So that

their integrity could be known.

8. Rasad (रसद): These were the spies, who did not care for their close friends and relatives. They could even poison any one. They were kept so that they could convey secret information about their close relatives to the king.

9. Parivarajika or Bhiksuki (परिव्राजिका अथवा भिक्षुकी): They were poor, matured, old men, widows, who had reputation in the mahals among the queens. They would go to the houses of the ministers/high officials too with a view to know their resources and integrity etc.

These spies should be appointed after checking up their family background, their knowledge of languages; the topography of various places; their way of dressing themselves; their capability of working incognito, their knowledge of the trade where they were posted and should be posted in their own country, at the residences of ministers, purohit, army commander, yuvaraj, escorts, in mahals, cantonments, with collectors, subedars, armymen, fort rakshaks, forest officers, etc. They should be posted to take care of their cooking, taking bath, messaging the body, bed-spreading, barber work, water carrier, and also near their houses as beggars, infirm, lunatics, dumbs, tribals etc. They can be males or females and should keep a watch on each of their movements. Kaptic student spies should frame their own signals to apprise others concerned and the raja of the deficiences noted by them. This would indicate that codal language was also in use in those days. Even the spies could not know each other. This was the secrecy maintained.

The spies had been posted at the places of the governors too so that any plan to dethrone the king could be immediately known by him. The information sent by the spies in codal language was deciphered in Rajmahal. If three or more spies transmitted the same information, then it was taken as true and necessary further action was taken otherwise further enquiries into the information sent, were made to know the genuineness of the same. If contradictory information was sent by different spies, then matter was checked up and the spy sending wrong information was taken up and punished or removed from service. Spies were also posted at the places of jewellers and traders, arranging weights and measurements so that under-measurement was not resorted to.

The spies were also posted with the governors of other countries. There they used to get employment and work with them and used to report all matters of interest to their king. They were paid too by the alien authorities so that there was no doubt on their bonafides as also by the king. The families of such spies posted in other countries were taken care of by the king himself. Such spies were also posted with the kings, ministers and high officials of foreign countries.

In addition, the traders working in forts, at the international boundaries, sanyasis, gwalas, agriculturists were also engaged for doing the spying work for the king engaging them. They were also secretly paid by such king. The sanyasis and vanprasthis were engaged for spying work in forests. These people could recognise the spies posted by the enemies and would apprehend them and present them before the king for futher enquiries and extracting information out of them. In this way these persons were doing double job — one to take information for their king and another detecting the spies posted by enemy countries. Spies were also posted with Purohit, Ministers and Prime Minister. These spies would mix up with general public and keep their eyes on the dignitaries for whom they were posted. These dignitaries could not, therefore, know their individuality. In this way every one had been alert thinking that he would be under watch by some spy from some corner and did not enter into wrong-doings. The spies also worked at the places of melas, gatherings to extract any information out of the discussions at those places. At such places, these spies start talking with one another, saying:

1. The raja is known as very capable but nothing outstanding is noticed in him. He rather extracts money out of the people after punishing and harassing them and in this way could detect the feeling of the people in respect of their king.
2. They also appreciated the king in such gatherings so

that people also started appreciating him.

3. They could know the rumours in public about governance and would suitably oppose the same and mitigate such rumours.

4. The people, who were satisfied with the governance, were recognised as such and those who were not happy were asked to tell the reasons for their not being happy and remedy the same so that none was unhappy in the kingdom. If they were still not satisfied, then they would make others criticise them and develop enmity with them, who would ultimately kill such people. So without the king coming in the dispute, the people themselves would eliminate such people and since this had been done at the instance of the punishing authorities themselves, their killers were not answerable to such authorities for such crimes. Since such people could even coroborate with the enemies, their elimination is desirable.

5. Very brave and capable persons could be kept by the king on his side by honouring them in public. Such honours are even now granted to deserving persons, who have done some outstanding job in any sphere.

6. The spies of the enemies could be detected by the king's men acting in similar way.

7. The spies posted in others' land were required to work there as per policy of appeasement or on monetary consideration to bring round the people on their side. If they could not be brought to their view by the above policies, then the policies of punishment and division should be adopted and continue telling the bad points in the governance of the enemy king so that they became indifferent.

8. After having brought round to their views, in their own country as well as in foreign countries, the spies should advise construction of forts in their country and start working for alliance or belligerence as warranted by the situation. All this should be done secretly. The place for such consultation should be in isolation so that others

may not know about it. Even birds were not allowed to listen to such talks. This might be in view of the fact that in ancient times, the parrots worked as spies and could convey information to the raja's men. Only authorised persons should join such talks and if any body spying there is caught, he should be finished then and there.

9. The talks could be known even by the movements of the people. The spies should, therefore, control their movements till the talks are started and at the same time keep a watch on others.

10. Even the king had to take a lot of care in respect of spies as:

    (i) An addict drunkard should not be engaged for consultations as under the influence of alcohol, he would divulge even the secrets.

    (ii) The king should not keep his men with him while having very secret talks with other kings as such persons could divulge the secrecy elsewhere. Similarly the conclusions with the men of other rajas by the spies, should not be leaked to others by the raja.

    (iii) The Raja should have consultations on secret matters with minimum possible persons as there would be more chances of leakage if many people could know the secrecy and in that case it would not be possible to fix responsibility on anyone for the leakage.

    (iv) Any decision arrived at in secret talks should be immediatley brought into action as the delay can cause leakage of the same.

    (v) The number of persons to execute any job should be fixed according to their capability.

    (vi) Besides keeping the spies in the houses of ministers, governors, the raja should fix spies to keep a watch on his sons and even wife (wives) with a view to know if the wife (wives) had been leaking out some secrecy to others or the sons were planning to uproot the raja. In case of any such thing happening, he should get the matter enquired and take remedial measure, including the death of wife/son.

(vii) The revenues of exchequer are out of the realisation of taxes. The raja should post spies at suitable places to save the revenues from being misappropriated or embezzled. They should keep watch on the collection of revenues and their proper accountal and apprise the raja in case of any deficiency. The spies detecting misappropriation/embezzlement should be rewarded by payment of one sixth of the detected money as reward so that the spies were encouraged in detecting more and more such cases. After all such detections even involve risk of life to the spies. This practice is even now prevailing in Customs, Police Departments.

(viii) There were strict rules for proper weights and measures and the raja's men kept a watch on their correctness with traders. The delinquents were severely punished.

The government employees were there for each department. For forts, mines, jungles, trade centres, there were employees to collect taxes under the overall supervision of 'Samharta'. The Samharta used to maintain record of topography, land area and population of each village in his books, where the boundary of each village was also indicated, there was also indication of residential areas, farming land, land for the army. Each village was under a 'Gopa', who kept the record of his village. Under the control of Samharta, some men in the villages were fixed as spies, who kept the accountal of the production, census of each varna and incoming and outgoing persons of the village. These spies also kept a watch lest any spy of enemy started living in the villages. Similarly the spies living as trade men used to keep a watch on the sales, production of raw material from mines, production from water tanks, farms, forests and their evaluation. They also kept a watch on imports and exports via sea and land routes and payment of cess on the same to government exchequer. The spies posted as tapasvis kept a watch on farmers, grazers, traders whether they declared the productions honestly. The pupils of these tapasvi spies kept a watch on temples, sarais, pilgrimage spots, as to who came there and for what purpose and that there was none from the side of the enemy.

In this way the Samharta managed his block properly, and on the basis of reports received from all Samhartas, the governance of the kingdom was carried out. The culprits detected by the Samhartas were presented before the raja, who decided suitable punishment—monetary or corporal—commensurate with the guilt involved and so everyone kept alert lest he was also caught by government employees.

Like Samharta caring for the block of villages, there were 'Nagrikas' appointed to take care of the affairs of the towns. The towns were divided into parts and a watch was kept on all movements in the towns like the Samharta doing in villages. Also for keeping a watch on forts, gardens, workshops, there were inspectors and spies. A list of such persons was prepared as were overspending or overdrinking and then enquiry was conducted about their resources. Wherever the resources created were by foul means, necessary action was taken against them. It was also seen whether any person was getting treatment for injury caused due to some armaments as such persons could be belonging to enemies. Every family head had to report to the 'Gopa' about any person coming to his house or going from his house. If such new comers committed theft during the night, then the house-owner, where new-comer had been staying, was held responsible. In this way, the residents were protected from any theft or robbery etc. Similarly proper watch was kept on undesirable elements wandering about as traders, grazers, gwalas, woodcutters in forests, people visiting temples, pilgrimage centres, storing drugs and narcotics, suspicious characters and anyone so detected was handed over to the authorities for enquiry and proper punishment. People causing any irregularity and mismanagement were also caught by the spies and handed over to authorities like:

1. In case of fire, if anyone did not try to extinguish, such person was punished.
2. Anyone, throwing rubbish on roads, was punished.
3. Anyone, creating obstacles in travelling on highway, was punished.
4. Burning wood was prohibited in summers and anyone violating this rule was punished.
5. Persons working with furnaces like blacksmiths, were settled at one corner of the town and starting such job at other places was punishable.
6. Anyone easing at highways, pilgrimage centres, wells, water tanks or near rivers was punished.
7. Anyone, leaving the dead snake, cat, dog in town, was punished.
8. There was fixed route for taking the dead persons and any one, taking from other routes, was punished.
9. Anyone wandering about in suspicious way during night was punished after checking up his antecedents.
10. Rape was punishable severely.
11. Every citizen was duty bound to inform the 'Gopa' or Samharta about any person with suspicious character or stranger. If any one did not follow it and his fault came to light then he was punished.

In this way the spies were responsible for keeping the environ clean and detecting the criminals. People found violating the rules were punished. Constant watch was also kept on the prisoners and those convicts, who could be reformed, were released on the recommendation of the Jailors. Such check up was exercised every fifth day.

There was such a net of spies that people thought that like omnipresent God, spies too were omnipresent and everyone thought that some watch must be kept on him everytime by someone and so he did not commit any crime.

As already indicated, the raja was also duty bound

to protect the people from foreign aggressions. For this purpose, Chandra Gupta Maurya had been keeping an army with elephants, cavalry, chariots and on foot. This army was very strong and disciplined. With the help of this army only, Chandra Gupta could become an emperor of a vast empire from a small kingdom of Magadha only. The extent of empire at the death of Chandra Gupta is not exactly known but it is certain that Ashoka had added only Kalinga and after that he had given up fighting and Ashoka was the emperor of the vastest empire ever had by any king in India. This included present India, Pakistan, Bangladesh and Afghanistan. It would indicate that Chandra Gupta too would be having that much empire except Kalinga. Such a vast empire could be created with the help of the spies and a strong army and could be governed too most effectively with the help of the chain of spies in every nook and corner of the kingdom. Chandra Gupta could know the happenings in other countries through his spies and what was happening in his country was not known to other countries as Chandra Gupta's spies were so sharp that they would apprehend any spy from alien country and punishment for such spies was death. Therefore, firstly the persons from other countries did not come for spying job to India and if anyone came, he was not able to do his job due to constant fear of being caught. In this way after knowing the position of other countries through his spies, Chandra Gupta invaded other countries and was able to easily conquer and then annexed it in his kingdom. The spies were also posted in army so that the army was not able to rebel.

Every government job was kept so secretly during Chandra Gupta's period that even Chandra Gupta himself did not sleep for two nights continuously at one place and he only knew where he would sleep the next night. We cannot think of any spies net-work, better than what Chandra Gupta had arranged, anywhere else. Such arrangement was made by Chandra Gupta under the guidance of Chanakya and it was continued during the reign of subsequent Maurya rulers too. Even Ashoka, who had become benevolent after Kalinga war, dealt with the criminals, detected by spies in his kingdom, very severely. If we minutely see, we would find such arrangement even today but who is able to take action and to what extent, is also known to everyone.

Magasthanese had come to India during Maurya period. He speaks of Indians as a remarkably law-abiding people and observes that crime was very rare. During Maurya time, the Police department had become a well-established administrative institution. The Arthshastra advises the imposition of stringent curfew for about two and half hours after dusk. The crime situation was tackled through Police officers, Garrison Commanders, soldiers and secret agents, who served as detectives. 'Danda' symbolises the coercive power of the state adequately buttressed by a moral and spiritual application, and was the first basic postulation responsible for the birth of Police system during that period. The Vedas, Samritis, the Buddhist and Jaina religious scriptures, besides the great epics, adequately mention the protection of subjects as the most important duty of the king.

Kautilya, who canonised an elaborate system of policing and laid down several grades of bureaucracy, could rightly be called the father of modern concept of Police. The traditions set by Kautilya were followed throughout the history and all over India. This system was maintained by Gupta rulers and their successors in northern and southern India. The Mahabharata considers the concept of 'Danda' as the upholder of religion and the prime duty of the king i.e. the protection of people is what was propounded by the early Arthashastra writers. If 'danda' was absent, the people would sink into tense darkness and when 'danda' moves about, the people do not fall into confusion provided it is directed well. Without danda, no student would study; no cow could be milched; no maiden could be given in marriage, all barriers would break down and the sense 'this is mine' would be lost. Danda destroys enemies and annihilates criminals from the kingdom. Subsequently with the growth of states, the kings' attribute of 'danda' was carried on by armed forces for preserving internal security and protection from external aggressions.

The policing system of Kautilya was on two distinct basis i.e. civilian departments entrusted with Police powers and the cadre of regular Police officers. Keeping in line with the general tenor of Arthshastra formulations, Kautilya has conferred Police powers on almost all departments that had public dealing. The hard core was composed of three tier system constituted by Pradesta for the rural areas and the Nararaka in urban areas at the top; the urban 'Sthanikas' in the middle and urban 'Gopas' at the bottom. Police headquarters were located in the capital with representative Police officers in all principle centres and important villages. Kautilya has not only placed the responsibility on central and district administration for the prevention of crime but also lays down that the people in the rural and urban areas are by and large answerable to the crimes committed within their respective areas.

After Ashoka, the Indian history enters a comparatively darker period for five centuries until the rise of imperial Guptas, except for a short period of rule of Kanishka. It was a period of foreign invasions and internal dissensions. Our knowledge of post-Maurya administrative system is rather meagre and only stray references are available. Only the Kusanas were a link between Mauryas and Guptas. They sought to perfect an administrative machinery by intermingling the traditions of India and the political ideas, which they inherited from Central Asia. The terms 'Mahadandanayaka' and 'Dandanayaka' occur for the first time in Kusana records. These are also found in Allahabad pillar inscriptions and other epigraphies. The Kusanas gave all important posts of 'Dandanayakas' and 'Mahadandanayakas' to their relatives.

As already indicated Ashoka's empire was the vastest ever held by any emperor in India. It included present India, Pakistan, Bangladesh and Afghanistan. Such a vast empire could be properly governed with the help of a net of spies in India and abroad as per Chanakya's policy narrated in Arthshastra. After Maurya dynasty, the important emperor was Kanishka. He too followed the tenets of Arthshastra, including the net work of spies. As Maurya dynasty declined due to non existence of a capable king succeeding Ashoka, so was the case with Kanishka too, when again the successors were mild and did not have the net of able spies.

After Kanishka, India was divided into small kingdoms. Then came the advent of Gupta period with Chandra Gupta as the first emperor. He also established his kingdom comprising of entire northern India and Afghanistan. In Gupta period, Chandra Gupta, Samudra Gupta and Chandra Gupta II (Vikramaditya) were the important rulers, who ruled the country from 320 A.D. to 415 A.D. After that, the country again started disintegrating. We get the information about Gupta rule from Fahien, a Chinese traveller, who visited India during that period. He has written that people were very prosperous. They did not have to report about the inmates in their houses as was the practice during Maurya period. There was no crime nor had anyone to go to Magistrate. People could travel on high-ways without any fear. Anyone could live in the town and could leave the town, whenever he wished so. There was no system of corporal punishment nor was there death sentence in existence. Punishments were awarded on pecuniary basis. This was in contradiction of what existed in Maurya period. There were 'Dandnayakas' in regions and towns and above them there was 'Mahadandnayaka' in the capital, who controlled the Dandnayakas. Similarly in governance there were Pratiharas and Mahapratiharas, who looked after the law and order in the kingdom. There were also Amatyas in provinces and Kumaramatyas in the capital eversince Ashoka's time. The Kumarmatyas were generally from royal house and they used to keep a watch so that there was no rebellion in the province and further spies were posted to oversee lest the Kumarmatyas should rise in rebellion against the king. In this way there was centralisation as well as decentralisation in governance. Similarly in every district and sub district too there were Ayuktas and spies posted. There was a Gopika in the village and all crimes committed in the village were settled by the Gopika there itself. The Gopika was also authorised to award punishment to anyone found guilty.

So far as the awarding of punishment is concerned, in Gupta period, there was a comprehensive penal code but unlike Maurya period, corporal or capital punishment was not there. The punishment was generally pecuniary, wherever it had to be awarded although crime was negligible in that period. The spies and the law and order men were paid in cash and not in the form of grant of land etc. The army was strong and it is because of Samudra Gupta being himself a brave and enterprising person and with the strong army, that he could conquer entire northern India. He also conquered the kingdoms in southern area but rather than annexing them in his empire, he kept them as vassal states. He had also held Aswamedha yagyas in which the emperor's suzerainty was accepted by all the vassal states. There was no rebellion in his time as he had a vast net of spies posted in his kingdom as also in his vassal states, although the vassal states had been given autonomy in internal governance. The spies used to keep the emperor informed of the minutest happenings in the state, detected criminals and got them punished. Since people were generally honest and prosperous, there was practically no crime and accordingly no law and order problems. This period has, therefore, correctly been called the golden period of Indian history.

During Gupta period, besides the continuance of combined police, military bureaucratic machinery, Police officers of higher echelons do not figure either in contemporary literature or the epigraphy. These duties might have been given to military detachments, who were stationed in different zones. Thefts were attempted by disperadoes, who committed dacoities and carried away cattle and property. They could be effectively controlled by militia or military force resulting in almost annihilation of crime.

The judiciary and police were two most important wings of the state administration. In Vedic period, when states were small and the king was directly administring justice, police was an integral part of the system. But with the passage of time, police responsibilities widened and a different organisation had to be created. Manu's police is divided into two functional departments viz the Criminal Investigation

Department and the Law and Order Wing. The Criminal Investigation Department is further divided into crime branch and special branch. The crime branch had two fold responsibilities viz collection of criminal intelligence and investigation of crimes and the special branch was entrusted with the task of collecting intelligence for the security of important dignitaries, prevention and protection of economic offences and undertook espionage. Manu calls the city police chief as 'Nagar Rakshadhikrita'. He advised the king to post in every city an officer exalted in position and imposing in appearance like the planet among the stars. He is mentioned as 'Nagar-raksha-dhikrita' in Sudraka, Nagarakh in Arthshastra and Nagarika in Gupta's Kalidasa. He was not only responsible for crime control but also pursued the rebels. Policemen were detailed to watch the rendezvous of anti-social elements such as lodges, water houses, sweet-meat shops, hotels, inns, brothels, theatres, vacant houses and town outskirts. They were watched by batches of stationary policemen and secret agents.

The villages in ancient India have enjoyed autonomy since the Vedic period and the system was hardly disturbed by the great rulers seeking to establish imperial authority. Even Arthshastra strongly advocated their retention. After the fall of Mauryas, however, none of the governments, established at different regions of India, thought of carrying their interference too far while constant wars and turmoils forced the people themselves to assume local burden and to discharge the duty of village watchmen. Principles of internal security, the moral and ethical responsibilities of the king and the system of policing, developed in ancient towns and villages, were effectively followed and improved by the successive Hindu kings. They were suitably advocated by the ancient Indian legal canons and literary population.

Kautilya's Arthshastra is the earliest exhaustive account of administration in ancient Indian society as also valid in certain aspects during Gupta period. The general administrative system as prescribed in Arthshastra was built round the collection of revenues. The Chief Executive Officer of the state — the Collector General — was responsible for collection of revenues as also for general supervision over most other departments of the administration. He had under him three commissioners of divisions, the latter in turn had under them the Nagarikas, in-charge of administration of cities and towns. The counterpart of these Nagarikas during the Muslim and early British rule, were designated as Kotwals. There was an elaborate system of maintaining a careful check on the movements and activities of all the inhabitants of a city through petty officers called Gopas, who also collected revenues.

Arthshastra gives details about exhaustive anti-corruption and surveillance machinery to keep a check against misuse of power and authority by officers.

1. Punishment to be meted out to erring officers.

2. Definitions of robbery, theft, defamation, assault, culpable homicide not amounting murder, and murder and punishment for these and other offences like rape, homosexuality, bestiality, sodomy etc.

In Gupta period the administration of cities devolved upon the officer called 'Kottapal'. This officer may be considered as the precursor of the 'Kotwal' of Muslim period.

After Vikramaditya, Guptas' rule started declining and the kingdom became shorter and shorter because of the weak successors. Still the dynasty continued till the end of sixth century.

We do not have a strong king after the fall of Gupta empire except Harsha, who succeeded in 612 A.D. The information about his period is available from the books written in his time by Bana, and the Chinese traveller Hiuen Tsang. He himself too had written Harsh Charitam. Harsh took interest in proper administration, justice, and public welfare jobs. He had also kept Ayuktas and Upayuktas in provinces and districts. They kept the king posted with latest information pertaining to their respective areas. Still there was not that much peace in his period as it was in Gupta period as the condition had deteriorated after Guptas' rule. Hiuen Tsang himself had been caught by a group of dacoits but a sudden storm saved him from their clutches. The penal code of Gupta period was used in Harsha's period too. Although, there was no capital punishment, yet life imprisonment was awarded for crimes against government or otherwise. On the charge of theft, at first pecuniary punishment was granted and on repetition, corporal punishment by cutting one hand and then on third time, the cutting of other hand was awarded. In this way the punishment in Harsha's time was severer compared to that of Gupta period but it was still mild compared to what had been prescribed in Arthshastra in view of the escalation in crime during Harsha's period. For social crimes, pecuniary punishment was generally awarded. Of course it was followed by corporal punishment on repetition of crime. The life and property were fully protected. For this, the king's armed men and spies had been having rounds of the areas entrusted to them. There were no thefts or dacoities in villages. There was no registration of the incumbents in houses nor there was the custom of bounded labour. Vyas Samriti, Brihaspati Samriti, Narad Samriti and Katyayan Samriti were written during this period. These are the reflections of how comprehensive Indian penal and other codes were. It had became easier and uniform to try any criminal and award punishment as per the provisions in these samritis.

The court of the emperor was the highest court of trial and punishment. It was also called the sabha or dharmsthana and the emperor was called Dharmadhikari. The emperor awarded punishment for the crimes in consultation with the members of the sabha. Proper investigation was got conducted before awarding punishment so that punishment to a wrong person was not awarded. The operations in this connection were that at first the criminals were apprehended by the armed men of the emperor or by his spies. They were presented before the competent authority with a charge-sheet. Then they were given a chance to defend themselves and after examining the defence and the witnesses produced, further investigation was got done, if need be; and then after such investigation, punishment was awarded. Then there were appellate authorities; the highest appellate authority being the emperor. The emperor's judgement was considered unbiased and correct. Even now somewhat similar procedure is adopted in the so called most efficient judicial system introduced by the British. As per Narad Samriti, there are four stages of the process, more or less as indicated above. At first FIR was filed, then it was seen under which section of the code, the crime fell, then the defence of plaintiff and defendant was taken and examined; then evidence/witnesses were examined and then the judgement was announced. The crime was to be proved by the plaintiff and the defendant gave his defence and produced witnesses. Punishment was awarded only after full satisfaction. Law of Torts was also in existence in ancient India although today it is accepted as a modern system in western countries only. There was punishment (pecuniary) even for libel, rebuking or defamation. Proper watch was kept on weights and measurements and under-weighment was severely punishable. Punishment was also there for gambling, drinking, rape etc. All these punishments could be awarded only after the criminals were apprehended. For this purpose the net of spies and armed guards was very effective during Harsha's time.

After Harsha again due to weak links of successors, the Harsha's vast kingdom got divided into small kingdoms. Then there was the advent of Rajputs, who were rulers of smaller kingdoms and had been fighting within themselves. For them their own kingdom was the country and there was no feeling of the country (India) as a whole.

At that time, Islam had come up in Saudi Arabia and fanatic Muslims had been after spreading Islam in the entire universe. They started invading in the West as also in the East. Europe (most part), Middle East, Africa, Western and Central Asia had been conquered by Muslim rulers and made Islamic. They also saw India divided into small kingdoms, whose kings had always been fighting within themselves. Then there was also the richness of the country, which had been known throughout the European and Middle East countries. Muslim rulers, therefore, had an eye on Hindustan. The Rajput rulers did not help each other even against the foreign invaders, rather they became happy, when Rajput ruler was subdued by a foreign aggression till it came on him too. There was no united fighting, rather sometimes the foreign invaders were invited to attack India and for this purpose even assistance was provided. The Rajput rulers also lacked the spying system and were caught unawares by the Muslim invaders, who invaded after checking up the position of the power of the invaded raja, the topography of the region, the armaments available through their spies, who came as merchants and took all secrets and then invaded having prepared accordingly. On the other hand, the Indian Rajput rajas had no spies and did not care to adopt the war strategies of the Muslims having seen them in several battles. They took battles as 'Dharamyudha', a concept far left behind by the universe. So the Rajput rulers were taken by surprise. Mohammed Gazni came to Panjab and then to interior places and went upto Somnath temple in Gujrat without any opposition by any king. He came seventeen times and took away lot of wealth from India so much so that once Mohammed Naurin reached Sind and Buddha monks helped him and supplied him eatables and other necessities so that they were not killed. The Muslims used to kill many Buddhas/ Hindus, made many as slaves and converted many to Islam. Once the Buddha monks even conspired with Muslim invader against their raja itself. Later on too Mohammedans made alliance with the nobles against their kings. This shows the vigilant and careful eye of Muslim invaders, who had taken help from their spies and the nobles of local rajas and Rajput rajas did not care either to unitedly give a fight or to bring themselves up to their level in armaments. The Raja Dahar of Sind faced the Muslim invader but his commander cheated him and made alliance with the invader. Therefore, the rajas did not keep an eye even on their nobles. Similarly the Prime Minister of Brahmnabad left his Raja Jai Singh and made friendship with the Muslim invader and the praja too helped Mohammedans out of fear.

This could be possible only when the rajas' spies were not working at all that the raja could not get any information about his own men making alliance with the invader.

Similarly in the case of Mohammed Ghori too, he invaded several times but was defeated by the strong king Prithvi Raj. Subsequently when Prithvi Raj kidnapped Jai Chand's daughter Sanyogita and married her and was amidst merry-making, that Ghori attacked and caught him unawares, possibly on invitation by Jai Chand, who was not happy with Prithvi Raj kidnapping his daughter. Rajputs were not well-versed with battle techniques. Prithvi Raj had changed from elephant to horse amidst the war and his men, taking Prithvi Raj as captured, fled and so he was defeated and killed by Mohammed Ghori. Prithvi Raj defeated him several times but neither killed him nor his people so that they did not dare attack again but just allowed him to go and come again with better preparations. Might be these Rajput rajas were over confident about their bravery but having seen Mohammedans already looted a lot, they should have been beware of their tactics.

6 MOHAMMEDAN PERIOD

Mohammed Ghori established his kingdom in India in 1192 and left his lieutenant Qutab-ud-din Aibak to rule over India. After Ghori had died in 1206, Qutab-ud-din declared himself independent sovereign Sultan of India. He also conquered several regions and annexed in his kingdom. He also followed the policy of attracting the ministers/commanders of rajas to his side and then defeated their rajas. The Slave Sultans continued but each time a Sultan died, the new one had to face the rebellious Hindu kings of various provinces, who used to declare themselves independent. Therefore, the first job for any Sultan was to subdue the rebel rajas. Balban took over in 1265 and saw that his governors/rajas had been rebelling everytime there was a change in the Sultanate or even in between. He, therefore, thought that the spies department had to be vigilant to avoid recurrence of such incidents and also he would have to treat such governors/rajas with a very heavy hand. He, therefore, posted his confident spies with the governors; with his ministers and nobles and at short distances in his entire kingdom. He also posted news-writers and news-carriers at every town/village and on the highways. They reported the matters direct to the Sultan. He also appointed spies in all departments so that there was no cheating or misappropriation or embezzlement of funds by wrong accounting etc. Anyone, not doing his duty, was killed so that others might learn a lesson. If there was any unreported incident in the kingdom, the spy fixed there was taken up. In this way the news-•writer had to keep a vigilant eye in his area. Once on a news-writer not having reported a plan against the King by the Governor of Badayun, he had been hanged.

Balban's strength was his army. He started paying them cash rather than allotment of land so that they did not involve themselves in the settlement of land but devoted to their jobs. There were robbers in abundance in and around Delhi. They used to rob the traders, industrialists and travellers so much so that the city gates used to be closed in the evening. In this way, there was insecurity in the public. The situation was worse in other provinces of Bengal, Bihar, Rajasthan. Even the petty nobles used to resort to robbing to fill their coffers along with the dacoits. Although it was a very difficult job to suppress them but Balban undertook to finish this insecurity in public. He started apprehending them with the help of his army and awarded severe punishment. Ferocious Afghans were posted at all places and highways and in this way the area around Delhi was first made peaceful and bereft of robbers. Then he took up the job in respect of other provinces too. The public was too happy for such an action of Balban. If we see through the provisions of Arthshastra, it would appear that introduction of spies' net-work, payment of salaries to troops in cash and dealing with the criminals with a heavy hand, were all there and may be someone in Balban's darbar would have advised him so.

Balban distributed the kingdom into provinces and districts and appointed brave officers at each place, who got the jungles and villages too cleared of robbers and dacoits. He established, for the first time, Police chowkies at short distances and posted armed men on those chowkies. He also posted news-writers and news-carriers under the overall control of the Mamalik. In provinces too, officers and Mamaliks had been posted. In case of any robbery, the Mamalik of the area was held responsible and punished. This was necessary to remove the anarchy in governance. Police chowkies and news-writers had been posted on highways too to ensure safe travel. Balban ruled for forty years because of the net of spies and strict punishment to criminals.

As usual, after Balban again slave rulers' chain came to an end due to weak successors. Then Khiljis appeared on the scene. They had not come from abroad as conquerers but were out of the sardars in India or their sons.

Ala-ud-din Khilji was the most important ruler of this dynasty. As already indicated, with the death of each king, there was chaos and anarchy in the kingdom and each governor used to declare himself independent. So, each king had to at first establish himself by suppressing the rebellions by governors. So was the position after Balban. Ala-ud-din found that the main reasons for such a situation were:

1. Ineffective spies' net as a result of which the king did not get the information about planning of his governors and other nobles against him.
2. Due to drinking, people used to get together and since it involved huge expenditure, people earned money by foul means.
3. The nobles too had get-together in inter-marriages and then planning to uproot the king.
4. Extra richness with some people also encouraged rebellions.

He, therefore, issued following 'Farmans' :

1. He confiscated all lands allotted for religious purposes and as 'mufti'.
2. He organised the spies' net and appointed news-writers, news-carriers and other spies. They had been posted at the places of all high officials, sardars, nobles, ministers, all towns, villages and high-ways. They collected information of use to the king and transmitted the same to him. This stopped whispering of any plots amidst the sardars/governors etc., and had a fear lest they should be watched by spies.
3. He prohibited drinking. Even the king himself stopped drinking and anyone violating this order, was severely punished.
4. Social gathering of all sardars and nobles had been stopped and they were not allowed inter-marriages.
5. Hindu rajas mostly rebelled. So the king heavily taxed them as a result of which, they became very poor.

6. Ala-ud-din had to keep a big army so as to quell the rebellions. With a view to reduce the expenditure on army, he fixed prices of all essential commodities and introduced price-control system. Anyone not selling commodities at fixed price, could be apprehended by the spies and then he was heavily punished.

7. The spies also kept a watch on proper weights and measurements and persons involved in selling commodities under-weight were punished.

8. He introduced a new department under Dewane-Riyasat and another Shahane-Mandi to monitor, above arrangements, with many officials, who fed the king with all information.

9. In this way the king was successful in quelling external aggressions and internal rebellions.

10. He also finished the system of award of Jagirdars to his sardars and gave incentives to his loyal officers.

But such a system contined during Ala-ud-din's reign only and again disrupted after his death. This gave chance to Tughlaqs to come up. Ghayas-ud-din Tughlaq continued with the policy followed by Ala-ud-din Khilji. He protected the agriculturists' interest and introduced incentives to them. Rather than being strict with the sardars, he reconciled with them. The organisation of news-writers, news-carriers and spies was kept in tact, rather he gave them horses for quick action so that the king was able to receive the information about any happenings, immediately. He thus ruled peacefully. He was succeeded by his son Mohammed Tughlaq, who reduced the number of spies. He introduced token currency but due to proper arrangement of spies not being there, counterfeit coins had been made out. There were mints in every house and the treasury was full of base coins. The foreign merchants did not accept those coins in exchange of goods brought by them resulting in chaos in the trade. Thus the king declared those coins as illegal tender and ordered all such coins to be got ex-changed. In this way the exchequer got emptied. Several governors rebelled and the sardars and nobles became anti-king. There was nothing like good conduct in anyone. He also committed the other follies of shifting the capital as a result of which there was anarchy and chaos in governance. It was all due to there being no proper spies' arrangements. We have thus seen that, whenever there was efficient spies' net, there was peace and security in public and whenever there was looseness in this organisation, there was chaos and anarchy.

As already indicated, foreign Muslim rulers had always been keeping an eye on the political situation in the country and whenever there was looseness in governance, they would invade with a view to take wealth from this country. So at that time, Timur invaded and reached Delhi without any opposition. This was due to the fact that the governors, having declared independence, they could not individually face the invader and central force had become weak. Timur took away lot of wealth, killed lakhs of Hindus, enslaved another lakhs and converted lakhs into Islamism. So at that time, there was complete chaos in the country.

Lodhis came to power in such a situation. First Lodhi ruler was Bahlol Lodhi and then Sikander Lodhi. Sikandar Lodhi ordered all governors to maintain correct accountal of all revenue and expenditure and submit the same to the Centre, who kept the accounts of the entire kingdom. Any default in accounting was dealt with severely. He had also kept spies to keep a watch on the movements of all governors. Once some sardars made a plan to dethrone Sikandar Lodhi and enthrone his younger brother Fatehkhan. The king could know the plot through his spies. The plot failed and the plotters were severely punished and nobles had been expelled from the state. In this way the king put to their place all sardars and nobles and governors. He had also posted his spies in towns, villages and on the high-ways. These spies sent reports direct to the king so much so that the praja had started thinking that the king had some divine power because of which he was able to know all that had been happening in the state. He was not only good administrator but also granted justice as per Islamic law. There was proper law and order in his time and the public was prosperous.

After Sikandar Lodhi, Ibrahim Lodhi succeeded. He was not a very capable administrator and the governors had rebelled. Governor of Panjab invited Babar from Central Asia to invade India so that after defeating the king of Delhi, he could become independent governor of Panjab. Babar did come and defeated Ibrahim in the first battle of Panipat and became ruler of India in 1526 A.D., after having been defeated five times in the past. Babar could thus conquer because of the infighting of the governors and the Centre being weak. Further, the spying system strengthened by Sikandar Lodhi had become weak again during Ibrahim's time. Babar had, through his spies and with the help of governor of Panjab, checked up the position and had accordingly drawn war strategy. That is why inspite of Ibrahim's force being several times more than that of Babar, he lost the battle because of weak war-strategy. Babar could not, however, live long and died. Humayun succeeded. At first he became busy in restoring the lost territory. Then he distributed his kingdom amongst his three brothers and kept a part with himself. Because of this distribution, the centre became weak. Although he had put spies of his confidence in all provinces, who sent information direct to the king, yet the governors of Malwa, Gujarat, Bihar and Bengal rebelled. There was chaos in Panjab too. Humayun fled from India, yielding the throne to Sher Shah Suri.

Sher Shah was a capable war strategist. He surprised Humayun by sudden attack telling him that he was going to attack the Marathas, and as a consequence, Humayun had to go out from India. He ruled India from 1538 to 1554, when he died but during this short period, he had done marvels. He strengthened the spy system. He distributed the kingdom into provinces and provinces into districts/sarkars and posted Shiqdars in each sarkar and province under the Chief Shiqdar at the Centre and above them there were Chief Munsif and Chief Qazi. The Chief Shiqdar was responsible for law and order. In big cities, there were thanas under Kotwals. They used to try the criminal cases and punish the criminals too. There were army troops under these Kotwals. In this way it was the arrangement like the present day arrangement of Police Commissioner. The Sarkars had been divided into Parganas and one Shiqdar had been posted in each of the Parganas along with one Qazi and a treasurer. They were responsible for keeping peace in the provices. From Parganas, the cases could go in appeal to Chief Shiqdar. Sher Shah also provided for thanas in big villages and towns along with sainiks. They were responsible for maintaining law and order in their respective areas. The department of spies was under the Barid-e-Mamalik. After 1554, when Sher Shah died there was no capable successor. So Suri dynasty was over. Sher Shah Suri is known for proper governance and administration. He introduced the system of transferring the high officers after a fixed period so that no vested interest could be developed. These transfers were after 2-3 years in each Pargana and province. His revenue department was also well administered. As per his orders, his men were to be mild at the time of evaluation of the product but strict for realisation of the government dues. Compassion was shown at the time of famine or when crop failed. The spies had special instructions to see that the agriculturists were not harassed and such complaints were immediately heeded to and prompt action was taken to redress the grievance personally by the king.

At the time of Sher Shah Suri, many base coins were in currency, which had been made of brass instead of gold. He withdrew all coins made of mixed alloys of gold and brass and introduced coins of pure gold and small change was made of silver and copper and the spies kept watch on the small coins to see that these were not made locally by the people. Anyone in possession of base coins, was severely punished. The currency introduced by Sher Shah Suri worked well not only during the reign of Sher Shah Suri but also during Mughal period and later on during the period of East India Company. Sher Shah had posted his spies at all exchange centres and business centres to see that there were no base coins in use any-where.

Sher Shah's police management was simple and effective. According to Persian historians, this arrangement worked nicely. "The Shiqdar-e-Shiqdaran was responsible for maintenance of law and order. In villages, this responsibility was entrusted to local people under the gram mukhiya. For any theft taking place in the village, the mukhiya was held responsible. He was asked to apprehend the thieves within a fixed period and on his failure to do so, he was punished. "In this way the mukhiya made all efforts so that there was no theft, robbery or dacoity in his village or on the highway otherwise he was to be punished for the same" (Abbas). He further says that during Sher Shah's time, people were so much secure that the traders and travellers could deposit their belongings at the chowkies on the highway and slept peacefully without any fear.

Sher Shah constructed several highways for safe travel and provided police chowkies with armed men. This not only reduced crime but increased trade leading to the increase in government revenues. Grant Trunk Road from Peshawar to Calcutta (now Amritsar to Calcutta) is No. I highway even today. He had made proper arrangement of spies. His spies reported every happening to the king through dak chowkies. This checked any rebellion or creation of vested interest by any officer and the king was able to receive information even from the remotest corner of the kingdom. The department of police chowkies was under the Daroga-e-Dak chowkies and he also had under him many news-writers, news-carriers, sainiks. It is because of this organisation that there was complete peace and security in the country.

Sher Shah's army comprised of people from all religions but Afghans were posted at senior positions. His attempt had been to meet upto the lowest rank troops. This not only provided moral support to such sepoys but the king could also know the treatment of high officers meted out to them and the high officers used to be careful too. The king had posted his spies in the army too so that the army or any army officer could not rise in rebellion against the king. Fauzdars were posted in the army. They were king's own confidents. They not only fought devotedly but took care of the interest of the country too. The king even used to post his spies in the army of the enemy and the king used to attack the enemy after getting appropriate information from the spies about enemy's position. Sher Shah believed in doing the jobs expeditiously. It is because of such expeditious action taken in attacking the enemy that the enemy could not get sufficient time to prepare himself to face the attack and in this way he was conquerer before the enemy could awake.

After Sher Shah's death, Humayun again became the king of Hindustan in 1554 and died in 1556. Then there was the second battle of Panipat in which Hemu was defeated and Akbar became the king under the guidance of Bairam Khan. He consolidated and reconquered his lost territory. He married a Hindu (Rajput) lady and framed the policy of concilliation with Hindu Rajput rajas. He continued the chain of spies, kotwals as introduced by Sher Shah Suri and had a well established kingdom. After Akbar, Jahangir, Shahjahan and Aurangzeb became the rulers of India and they all continued the same spies arrangement. The emperor used to appear in person before public daily and himself listened to the public grievances and announced decisions then and there itself except in cases where the matter needed investigation, where investigation was ordered. In addition there was the arrangement of 'Gusalkhana', where the emperor had consultation with his senior officers/ministers and disposed off important matters. Also there was the system of 'Zenana' and 'Khilawat Khana' where the emperor met the spies and took decisions on secret and confidential matters. At such places only Diwan and Bakshi were allowed to be present. The emperor tried to be present on all these occasions. Such darbars were held even when the emperor was out on expeditions.

In emperor's council of ministers, there was one Chief Qazi and one minister for ecclesiastical affairs. Under them there were Muhtasibs. His job was to look into the religious matters in addition to seeing that there was no under-weighment, under-measurement or selling the essential commodities at high rates. He also ensured that the government land was not encroached upon. He was also responsible to see that no drugs or intoxicants were sold; no rapes took place; and no immoral activities took place. Gambling was prohibited in the towns. The restrictions imposed on non-Muslims were properly complied with, was also ensured by this officer.

Daroga-e-Dak chowkies, introduced by Sher Shah was still in vogue. Horsemen and runners were posted at short distances so that the dak could reach expeditiously. It is said that dak used to reach Hyderabad from Delhi within five days. It is because of this organisation that the emperor was able to check rebellions and eliminate crime from the kingdom. For ensuring the information reach the emperor expeditiously, there were.

1. Waqa-navis
2. Khufiya-navis and
3. Harkaras

In every block and big towns, there was a news-writer along with a Khufianavis and requisite number of Harkaras. In big towns of provinces, there were news-writers and his agents were appointed in districts, main towns and big villages. The Waqanavis used to send his report to the news-writer every week and the news-writer used to compile the same and send it to the emperor. Even the permanent staff could not know of these reports. These were received by Daroga-e-Chowki on behalf of the Emperor and presented before him. The Daroga used to read these reports to the Emperor in 'zenana' chamber. These reports were sent in hollow cylinders with their mouths sealed. The runners were posted at every three koses, who carried the dak to the next runner quickly and in this way the dak reached the destination.

The Daroga had the permission to send important dak to the king even in harem. Anyone creating obstacle or interfering in this work was severely punished.

During Akbar's time, the city administration had been streamlined and all important cities and towns were placed under direct charge of Kotwal. The provincial Kotwal was incharge of the capital city of the province. The Kotwal was also required to perform duties for the municipal administration in the city and also as a censor of morals of its inhabitants. The administration of the district headquarters town was also in the hands of an officer having the same designation viz. Kotwal. He also enjoyed the position of a Magistrate as far as criminal cases of the district headquarters town were concerned. As a consequence of engagement of Fauzdars by Muslims, the power and authority to administer justice rested in them but still the Zamindars as a class, did not prove their mettle in curbing crime and lawlessness. Each such specie was busy fending for himself and whatever strength, a Zamindar could acquire by maintaining a hand of lathials, either openly or on the sly, was used more for ensuring collection of revenues and oppressing the ryots. Seldom, if ever, was such might used for the safety and security of the common man.

Jahangir had issued twelve farmans for eliminating the crime from the kingdom and police was responsible for compliance of these farmans. These were:

1. The Jagirdar shall not for his own sake or in the name of "Mir bahari' impose/collect any cess.
2. The Jagirdars had to provide sarais and police chowkies at high-ways, where the thefts or robberies took place and police was posted at these sarai's so that the travellers were not looted.
3. The goods of the travellers were not opened on the way.
4. The police had to ensure that on anyone's death, his property went into the hands of his heirs and was not misappropriated by anyone else.
5. No one could either manufacture/produce or sell narcotics, drugs or liquor.
6. No one could keep anyone under detention.
7. The punishment of cutting ear or nose could not be awarded.
8. The Jagirdar or high official could neither encroach upon public land nor had cultivation of his own on it.
9. No Jagirdar could marry the girl of his own Pargana.
10. The jagirdars were obliged to provide hospitals in towns

and run the same with the revenues from government land.

11. The animals could not be slaughtered on some fixed days of the month.
12. The cases of all criminals, who had been in captivity for long periods, were reviewed and those, who had started behaving, were released.

The narration of Mughal period will not be complete without mentioning about the rule of Shivaji. Shivaji came up during the reign of Aurangzeb. He came out to face the Mughal empire with the help of a few Marathas. His spying system was responsible for his success. He went on conquering one fort after the other. He first used to collect information about the security men posted in the fort through his spies and would then attack suddenly. The government officers could not even know of it. Possibly the government officers never thought of such attacks and, therefore, did not care to post their spies for such jobs. Shivaji met Afzal Khan, who wanted to swoop him down but Shivaji could know of his intentions through his spies and went duly prepared and armed to meet him and before he could swoop on Shivaji, Shivaji killed him. Similarly, another officer, Shayasta Khan was sent to subdue Shivaji but here again after checking up his position, Shivaji attacked his residence on one night and he fled losing his fingers. His escorts and some other people were killed. Jai Singh was thereupon sent by the emperor. He entered into a treaty with him and agreed to meet Aurangzeb but Aurangzeb did not treat him well and he left his darbar. He was, however, caught and put in jail. From jail, he came out in baskets of sweets sent for being distributed as alms through a well-organised plot. Shivaji then established a Hindu kingdom (His dream). His spies department was fully alert and because of that only he could establish a Hindu rajya in Mughal regime. He expanded his territory by getting prior information through his spies and then suddenly attacked the place so that the enemy could not know of his movement or designs; meaning thereby that the spies department of Shivaji was superior to that of Mughals. He had also posted spies in his kingdom to detect criminals and getting them punished. Also all happenings in the kingdom were reported to Shivaji. In his ministers, there was one Minister-in-charge of spies department called Wazir-e-Vaqanavish. After collecting the reports from the spies, he used to present them before Shivaji. Shivaji himself too toured the kingdom incognito and after apprehending the criminals, punished them then and there. He used to punish his staff severely in case of non-performance. This made all his officers and staff quite alert in the discharge of their duties.

7 BRITISH PERIOD AND THEREAFTER

After Jahangir, Shahjahan succeeded and then Aurangzeb came in 1658. Aurangzeb died in 1707 leaving a vast empire comprising of present India, Pakistan, Bangladesh and a part of Afghanistan. It was difficult to control such a vast empire from Delhi. In his life time itself, therefore, Marathas and other rulers of South had started raising their heads and declaring independence. When Aurangzeb went to Deccan, northern India was left neglected. In this way Aurangzeb could neither control southern nor northern India. Such governance had been possible during Mauryas' period as their spies system was marvellous, whereas in Mughal empire, every governor had always been waiting to rebel, whenever centre was weak. Infact this had been continuing in India eversince the Muslim invaders came and established their rule as they could neither suppress Hindu king nor could tame the Muslim governors. Consequently within 40-50 years of Aurangzeb's death in 1707, the Mughal rule started dwindling. On one side, Marathas had been coming up and on the other, British had also put their foot on Indian kingdom after the battle of Plassy in 1757 and battle of Buxar in 1761, they had become a power to be reckoned.

Dutch, Portuguese, French and British had come to India for trade in early 18th century. Due to their infighting, they had started keeping some force and this force ultimately helped British in subduing Siraj-ud-daula in 1757 in the battle of Plassy although mainly the defeat of Siraj-ud-daula was on account of British having bribed his Commander-in-Chief, Mir Jafar to make him governor of Bengal if he managed the defeat of Siraj-ud-daula, this could happen only because Siraj-ud-daula did not have proper spying system. British and French had been fighting in Europe and its direct effect was on their Indian establishments too. There had been continuous piracy on seas too between these European nations.

In India Seth Amin Chand and Jagat Seth too became the treachery tools of British in the plot to dislodge Siraj-ud-daula. In this way India was sold out by Indians only to the British for pittance. Siraj-ud-daula, due to lack of spies, could not know the movement of armeda from Madras to Calcutta and plot of bribing Mir Jafar with the collusion of Jagat Seth and Amin Chand. Also poor war strategy too was responsible for defeat of Siraj-ud-daula. The enmity of Prithvi Raj and Jai Chand brought Muslims to India and treachery of Mir Jafar brought British to rule India. This also made the British wiser having known the weakness of Indians, who could easily be purchased by bribing them. Later on in Buxar battle; war with Sikhs; battle with Marathas, every where British became victorious by dint of their treacherous activities and lack of spying system of Indian Rajas/Nawabs. After Mir Jafar had become Governor of Bengal, his son-in-law Mir Qasim settled to pay the British heavily if he was made Governor of Bengal. So he was made Governor and subsequently again Mir Jafar was made the Governor. In this way making and unmaking of Governor of Bengal came in the hands of British and with every change, they got heavy amounts as the price of change. This made British's position stronger and Governor's position weaker in Bengal.

After battle of Buxar, British became powerful governors of the land. Warren Hastings came as Governor General of East India Company. He established civil and criminal courts in Calcutta and also provided Sadar Diwani and Sadar Nizamat courts. In Calcutta, a Mayor's court was also established. In these courts, Muslim law was allowed to be followed. In entire Bengal, dacoits' rule prevailed. They had the backing of big zamindars and ex-officials as they had been ousted by the British and they needed some source of income for defraying their inflated expenses. Hastings tried to suppress the dacoits. The dacoits were apprehended and were hanged in villages so that it may have deterrent effect on others. Their families were made slaves and their properties were confiscated. Another nuisance of that time was that of sanyasis. They wandered about naked in groups. They used to loot the travellers and others on high-ways and hided in jungles. Generally after looting the victims, they used to kill them too. Hastings used to call them 'Indian Gypsies'.

Hastings took some remedial measures as:

1. Fauzdars were appointed in 14 districts of Bengal to be responsible for protection of inhabitants by detection of and apprehension of all public robbers within the respective districts and for transmitting constant intelligence on all matters relating to the peace of the people in the Presidency.
2. Zamindars, farmers and other officers of the revenue collection were enjoined to afford the Fauzdars, all possible assistance in the discharge of the above duties and to obey such orders as they may issue in that connection.
3. Zamindars or farmers convicted of failure to assist the Fauzdar in the execution of his duties shall be responsible for any loss sustained by such misconduct.
4. All members of public found guilty of receiving fees or other pucuniary benefits from robbers, knowing them to be such, shall be adjudged criminals and punished with death.

Cornwallis, who succeeded Hastings as Governor General, is the innovator of an organised police administration in Bengal. The following important provisions were made by him:

1. The Police in the country is in future to be considered under exclusive charge of officers of government, who may be specially appointed to that trust. The land-holders and farmers of land, who keep up establishment of thanedars and police officers for the preservation of peace, are accordingly required to discharge them and landlords and farmers are prohibited from entertaining such establishments in future.

2. Landlords and farmers of land are not in future to be considered responsible for robberies committed in their respective estates or farms, unless it shall be proved that they connived at the robbery.
3. The magistrates are to divide their districts into police jurisdictions, each jurisdiction to comprise an extent of country not exceeding ten kosas square. The guarding of each jurisdiction to be committed to a daroga to be stationed in such a manner as to bring the principal towns, bazars, gunjes, and squares in the centre so that this police establishment may serve for the protection of these principal places.
4. The police jurisdictions are to be numbered and to be named after the central places.
5. The Magistrates are to nominate darogas in the first instance and to fill up all future vacancies. No daroga to be removed except on proof of misconduct.
6. Any person having a charge to prefer against another for murder, robbery, house-breaking, theft or other crime or offence cognisable by the criminal court, shall be at liberty to prefer in writing to the daroga of the jurisdiction in which the crime is committed.
7. The darogas are authorised to apprehend without charge and without issuing a 'dastuk' or writ, persons found in the act of committing a breach of peace or against whom a general hue and cry shall have been raised or who shall be detected with stolen goods. In other cases the darogas are prohibited from apprehending any person without a charge having been preferred against him in writing.
8. The daroga upon receiving the information of any notorious docoit or robber harbouring within his jurisdiction, shall apprehend him and forward him to Magistrate.

The rule also prescribed about the detailed description of other miscellaneous powers and duties of the darogas to discharge an accused in some cases on the basis of

'Razeenama' to be executed by both the parties.

Between 1792 and 1817, a large number of regulation enabling, repealing and amending, covering functions and activities of Police in Bengal had been passed in order to clear the ambiguities.

An important milestone in the history of policing in Bengal is the Fifth Report of Select Committee appointed by House of Commons in 1808 to enquire into the affairs of the Company. The report issued in 1812 devoted one section to deal with the state of crime and Police in Bengal. The Committee suggested:

1. Collectors should cease to exercise magisterial functions.
2. Districts should be divided into sub-divisions in each of which a Deputy Magistrate be posted with authority over Police.
3. The Thanedars/Darogas should be of three grades with pay Rs.100, Rs.75 and Rs.50 respectively.
4. Village chowkidari system should be recognised. The chowkidars should be better paid and responsibilities of the village officers should be clearly defined and enforced.

In view of the complicated procedure followed in courts during Mughal period, not many cases were filed in the courts. At that time severe punishment was awarded without properly investigating the matter. Hindu law was not known to British as the same was out of application during over 600 years of Muslim rule. Hindus, therefore, avoided knocking the doors of the courts. All criminal cases were decided in the courts as per the dictates of the politicians and dacoits. Zamindars gave refuge to the dacoits and in this way public had to suffer. Hastings, therefore, had started apprehending the criminals and getting them punished.

During Mughal period, there was no police administration in Bengal. Zamindars only engaged Pathans and other strong persons to maintain law and order as per their volition. The villagers had to supply the major portion of the agricultural products to the village chowkidars. Out of this, a portion used to go to these Pathans and the balance was for the zamindars. The village chowkidars too were a part of the dacoits. Hastings did not have any one except the army to suppress them. He appointed area fauzdars to suppress them but was not successful as neither any proof of dacoity could be obtained nor any evidence/witness was available as no one was prepared to stand witness for such robberies as every one was afraid of them. In 1781 Hastings removed fauzdars and appointed magistrates, who after investigation, used to present the case in the nearest criminal court. This resulted in the beginning of bribery in the courts. In Benaras and Lucknow, the residents had created a mess. They did not have any specified powers but in practice, they were the defacto rajas of their areas. To get rid of such people, Lord Cornwallis started Indian Government Service. He also increased the salary of the residents and they had been kept under the surveillance of the spies so that they did not harass the public. This involved extra expenditure but at the same time the bad deeds could be avoided.

Cornwallis desired to eliminate bribery and robbery. Through government officials and later on by the same policy followed by Wellesly, some success could be attained. But upto 1831, the structure of criminal courts continued to be same. In 1831, Lord Willian Bentinck saw these courts in a mess. He introduced circuit courts, which also looked after the jails. He also ordered periodical review of the inmates of jails. This way arrears of criminal cases could be reduced to some extent but the civil courts still had a lot of arrears. One reason for reduction in criminal cases was also the improvement in police organisation brought out by Lord Cornwallis. In 1792, he posted Superintendents of Police in each district, and after dividing the districts into thanas, he posted a daroga in each thana. The criminal administration of the district was placed under the district officer. Zamindars were not allowed to maintain police. In 1808, he posted Police Superintendents in three districts and having noticed good results in those districts, this system was introduced in other districts too in 1827. The same police system is continuing today too and is considered to be the best arrangement. In Bengal, however, this system did not suit in view of the special position of Bengal and continuance of dacoity in that province under the patronship of the zamindars. This situation continued in Bengal, particularly since police too feared those dacoits. In 1845, Lord Dalhousie saw these groups of dacoits increasing day by day. He deputed some persons naked in the jungles so that the dacoits could not get anything out of them and then caught them. Cornwallis made the civil courts accessible to all by allowing civil cases being filed there on less expenditure. He also carried out improvement in criminal cases rules. He appointed 28 judges in the districts and increased the number of circuit courts too. Appeals in civil cases could also be filed in the circuit courts. Under the circuit courts, there were several Indians working as Amins and commissioners, subsequently replaced by Munsifs. Europeans were posted as judges. Revenue cases were taken out from them and entrusted to Collectors. In this way the judges were left with court cases only and enabled quick disposal of court cases. Cornwallis prepared a penal code after carrying out improvement in judicial law. At that time, there was rush of cases in courts throughout the world but Bengal surpassed all as the zamindars did not allow smooth working of the courts.

Lord Clive by introduction of subsidiary system, had maintained army at the cost of the local rajas and nawabs. The British were able to maintain them at the cost of the rajas/nawabs, who were not able to meet these expenses as very heavy cost was charged for such army and this army could be used by the British for fighting against any raja/nawab. In this way, the expenses of their army were defrayed by the rajas/nawabs and the rajas/nawabs too had to maintain their own army. In view of the heavy expenditure on army, nothing was left for maintaining securitymen and this resulted in increase in the number of dacoities and robberies. Lord Wellesly stopped the subsidiary system and instead residents were posted in such territory and police was kept under them for maintaining law and order. The external affairs of these states were in the hands of British. The expenditure on the residents and police was borne by the respective states. British could use these policemen along with their army in case of need.

Lord Willian Bentinck posted as Governor General in 1828, remained here for seven years. He brought about improvement in social, educational, judicial and economic condition of the country. The law and order was still not up to the mark inspite of improvements brought about by Cornwallis and Wellesly. East India Company, which was a trading organisation, had now become ruler too. This involved extra expenditure to the company as the expenditure on law and order, which was so far borne by the states, now fell on the British rulers. It was, therefore, difficult for Bentinck to bring any improvement in this sphere. The expenditure had already gone high from Pounds one crore in the past to two and a half crores now with no corresponding increase in revenues. Bentinck, therefore, reduced expenditure on army and other staff.

No work was being done in provincial courts. Bentinck posted responsible officers in those courts. This resulted in some improvement in the working of these courts. The cases of inmates of jails were reviewed and the inmates, still continuing in jails without any reason, were released. The criminal courts had been wound up and their work was entrusted to District Collectors. This experience, however, was not successful and, therefore, the criminal cases were entrusted to District Magistrates, and Munsifs were posted under them for quick disposal of cases. Police was also kept under District Magistrates.

In this way the investigation and disposal of criminal cases, and jails were under one authority, the District Magistrate. He was able to do justice to all this work. Europeans had been posted as District Magistrates so that they could not involve themselves in corrupt practices in league with the local people. This eased the position in apprehending the dacoits and getting them punished as so far the zamindars were creating obstacles in elimination of these dacoits.

Having seen shortage of European officers after they had been entrusted with the disposal of criminal cases, Bentinck enhanced the jurisdiction of civil courts and posted Indian judges in those courts as Indian judges were paid less compared to European judges. This resulted in saving in expenditure. Apprehending the criminals and processing cases against them was more difficult than awarding punishment to them. Cornwallis had introduced thanedari system with Indian darogas and some sepoys under them and brought it under government control. The chowkidari system prevailing in the villages had worn out and so after eliminating this system, a regular force was created for this purpose. In England, metropolitan police system was introduced in 1829. Bentinck too on same basis introduced police system in big towns in 1830. This police force used to patrol the area and detect the criminals. The expenditure of such force was borne by the residents fixed on the basis of a set proportion. Subsequently this system was introduced in villages too, and in that case the expenditure was borne by the villagers. In this way, a police force became available without the government having to spend anything on them. This force was under the control of the government and maintained at the expense of residents. Simultaneously, the thanedari system also continued under government control.

There were many cheats and dacoits during Bentinck's reign. Thugs were hereditary professionals. They were also called 'Phansidars'. They used to catch the people in isolated places and looted them after killing them. They used to entrap the people in their own way and people too believed them. They were then taken at isolated places and killed and robbed. They were also the followers of 'Kali Goddess'. They used to sacrifice the people in Kali temples. They had the patronage of zamindars and a big portion of the loot went to zamindars. Entire north India was infested with such thugs.

Bentinck entrusted the job of eliminating them to Col. Sleeman by creating a department under him. After checking up their modus operandi, these persons were caught and got punished. According to Sleeman, these thugs were in thousands and it was a difficult job to eliminate them. Still within a few years, this thugee was finished.

Apart from thugs, there were many dacoits too and they too caught the people and robbed them. They used to visit villages in nights and looted them and went to their hiding places in jungles. They were in large number and it was also difficult to finish them as they had the patronage of big resourceful people. After British rule and abondonment of local army, the sepoys had all become dacoits. Even if they were caught, nobody came forward to give evidence against them out of fear and in this way they could not be punished and became more ferocious on acquittal. It was, therefore, difficult to eliminate them. More clever within dacoits, would after dacoity, sneak into the territory of neighbouring state from where they could not be apprehended being in other's land. In western India most of such dacoits belonged to Bhil community. Outram was deputed to finish them. He got them detected and punished and in this way got them finished. Subsequently they were eliminated from other parts of India too with a heavy hand.

Apart from thugee and dacoity, 'Maria' was another evil in those days. In this, the people were caught and sacrificed in temples. Being religious sentiments behind such evils, public rebellion was feared. Still after some time, such evil too was brought under control, although not completely finished even to date and we come across some cases of human sacrifice even in present days.

Along with 'Maria' there was another undesirable custom of 'Satee' in which the wife used to burn herself alive on the death of the husband on the same pyre. In most of the cases, such burning was by force. Since it was a social evil, and continuing since Vedic era, it was difficult to suppress it. It was more prevalent in Rajputs and there was fear of the public rebellion on its suppression, creating difficulty for the government. At that time, some social reformers came to help the government and with their help, it could be suppressed to some extent, although it is in existence even today to some extent. It increased during Muslim rule as with the death of Rajputs in battles, their wives did not want to fall in Muslims' hands. Therefore, they used to perform 'Johar'. The spies were alert and reported the incidences of Satee to the government.

In this way, many lives could be saved.

By 1855, the annexations in British territory were complete; the last annexed were Punjab in 1849 and Berar in 1853. Punjab was annexed by defeating Sikhs and Berar was handed over by Nizam to British as he owed lot of money to British on account of charge of contingent forces and since he was not able to pay this amount, he handed over Berar to British. Thus British made up their territory equal to about two-thirds of India by 1855. The annexations were on account of conquests from local rulers; annexation by rulers, who were not able to pay under Subsidiary Alliance System or payment towards charges of contingent forces lended by British to help the local rulers and by Doctrine of Lapse.

So far as the conquests are concerned, British could not face the local rulers openly. These were, therefore, by treachery such as in battle of Plassy, where Siraj-ud-daula was defeated by bribing Mir Zafar to manage the defeat of Siraj's forces in consideration of his being made Governor of Bengal. The treachery plan was made by Jagat Seth and Amin Chand on receipt of heavy amounts from the British. It could be possible as Siraj did not have adequate spying arrangements. He could not know the movement of armade from Madras and could not further know the plot against him by Mir Jafar, his Commander-in-chief, Jagat Seth and Amin Chand, whereas British could know through their spies in Siraj's kingdom, all his movements.

Subsequently, in the battle of Buxar too British got help from Mughal emperor in consideration of heavy amounts paid by British. Then in the Maratha wars, the main rajas were Scindhia, Holkar, Gaikwar, Bhonsle and Peshwa. Peshwa asked for help from the British and they extended the help on Marathas keeping British army in Poona at their expenses and thus British got a hold on Marathas and could know their movements by their spies. In subsequent war, Marathas were defeated by British because of an efficient spying system. They learnt Marathi language and remitted all information about Marathas' movement without their knowing it. Also the Marathas did not have their spies amongst British although Shivaji had created an efficient spies net.

In first Mysore war (1766), Nizam, Marathas and British formed a coalition against Haider Ali. He could not fight with all of them together. So he first disposed of Marathas and Nizam and then with the help of Nizam attacked British forces but was defeated because Nizam left Haider Ali and went over to the side of British. It could be because of the treacherous tactics of British and due to inadequate spying arrangement with Haider Ali as he could not know the change in alliance by Nizam from Haider Ali to British. British then made up peace with Nizam and entered into an alliance with Haider Ali. Haider Ali and British, however, continued fighting in second Mysore war. When Haider Ali died and Tipu Sultan took over, Tipu wanted to have revenge from the British in alliance with Nizam but by their efficient spying system, British could know of this alliance and they then won over Nizam to their side resulting in defeat of Tipu. In this way British got over Tipu by their efficient spying system and absence of the same with our rulers.

In Sikh wars, the first Sikh war with British took place in 1845, when Sikhs had been fighting for succession to the throne after Ranjit Singh's death. Sikh army, being very strong, had their say in the matter. Rani Jinda and Lal Singh ordered army to march on British. British feared the Sikh army. Sikh army crossed Satlej and attacked on British (after Satlej, British territory started). When Sikh army was likely to win, Lal Singh betrayed and had alliance with the British and so the Sikhs were defeated. Again during the second Sikh war too, Teja Singh, the commander, had alliance with British resulting in defeat of Sikhs. Then Gulab Singh became commander-in-chief but he too, for personal gain, plotted with British to manage Sikhs' defeat. In the battle, at first Teja Singh, who had been bribed by British, fled away from the battle, followed by Gulab Singh. In this way, British annexed Punjab by treacherous methods. This also shows that all British victories in India were :-

1. By making one raja fight against another.

2 By extending help to one raja against another and in this way getting a lot of money towards war damages or for contingent forces.

3. By treacherous methods as in battle of Plassy, Mysore wars, Maratha wars and Sikh wars.

4. By efficient spying system and fighting after ascertaining correct position of the enemy.

5. By devotion to East India Company and England. This was lacking in Indian rulers, who had no unity and their commanders, who had no integrity towards their masters; no proper spying system; no war strategy etc. compared to British.

During the Mutiny of 1857, there was not much disturbance so far as the administrative set up was concerned. Of course British had known that they would have to mix up with the local residents and could not trust the local officers any more. The British, therefore, set up an organisation of British officers in 1860 and posted British officers in each district with instructions to be on tows for maximum period. After this three kinds of administrative set up were introduced in districts. British were, however, able to suppress mutiny because of their efficient spying net-work through out the country:

1. In Sind, Punjab, Oudh and Nagpur, existing British officers were posted as Commissioners and 'Tarafdars'. These officers complied with the administrative instructions issued from time to time and enquired into criminal cases, if found necessary after proper investigation and also decided all civil cases. There was a workable Penal Code. The civil cases were decided by common sense based on customs, traditions and existing law. For rural districts, such principle only could be followed. John Lawrence has written "We have introduced such a system in which without any show off the plaintiffs and defendants are made to present in court along with their witnesses and after hearing, decision was given to them then and there."

2. In small courts of Bengal, Madras and Agra, cases were

made out only based on law and rules and then such cases were decided in district courts. The Collectors were lower in rank compared to the Deputy Commissioners of Punjab and in the areas of Zamindars, their position was still lower.

3. In British regime, Indian Penal Code, Criminal Procedure Code and Civil Procedure Codes were prepared. With these codes, the discretionary powers of the judges got reduced.
4. The district administration was not under one officer but under several officers. All district officers used to report directly to the Provincial Government and followed their orders.

In 1859, Robinson, a Madras civilian of high standing was appointed the Chief Commissioner of Police and directed to submit a scheme for the reorganisation of the police. The Commissioner observed:

"First, the police becomes a distinct department under the direct supervision of the government; its members of all grades being divested of judicial functions and being under the exclusive control and management of their own officers. Second, the administrative and judicial functions of the magistracy remains as at present. The police will execute all his lawful commands but will not interfere with the internal economy and arrangements of district management".

The Court of Directors was getting impatient at the inability of the Government of India and the Provincial Governments to come to grip with the problems of policing; its main concern having been to see a reformed system of criminal administration being brought into being in the Indian possession on the basis of the lessons of policing in England. A Police Commission was appointed in 1860 to:

1 Propose a new system of policing applicable to India generally, whereby economy and efficiency might be secured.
2. To prepare for publication, all available information

regarding the best system of police organisation.

3. To collect the most complete and comprehensive statistics obtainable regarding the cost and establishment of police of all kinds throughout India.

The Commission recomended inter alia—

1. The police under each local government or administration should constitute one force and be under an officer to be styled Inspector General of Police in whom should be vested control over the organisation; the responsibility of maintaining it in a state of efficiency by proper attention to its discipline, internal economy and its general management through its own officers.
2. In each district there should be an European Superintendent of Police, departmentally subordinate to the Inspector General of Police but required to obey the orders of the district officer in matters relating to prevention and detection of crime and preservation of peace.
3. In large districts, there should be an Assistant District Superintendent, who should also be an European officer to assist the District Superintendent of Police.
4. The subordinate police force should be composed of
   (a) Inspector of Police
   (b) Head constable and
   (c) Sergeants to be subordinate to Head constable and
   (d) Constables, who should be divided in three grades of pay.
5. The force in each district should be divided into appropriate police sub-divisions.
6. The head constable was to be incharge of police parties located at station house.
7. Wherever practicable, the men of the police force should be enrolled from the province in which they served.
8. Residential quarters should be provided for the police at the cost of the state and that accommodation for the

families of the police should be discretional with the local government.

9. Suitable but inexpensive uniform should be perscribed for all grades of police under each local government and the uniform should be furnished to all officers of police below the rank of Inspector at the cost of the State.

10. Village watchmen, being an ancient institution in India, it may not be desirable to dispense with it though many of them may not be of desirable category. Their remuneration was to be fixed by the district officer and they were to be under the order of the organised police.

Police Act of 1861 was introduced according to which Police structure was based on British model. Police was kept under one European District Police Superintendent and all government departments were placed under European officers. With this, there was a net of European officers in entire India.

Lord Curzon felt that the public was not satisfied with the provisions of 1861 Police Act. He, therefore, appointed Fraser Commission in 1902 to examine the police structure in India and give his suggestions to improve the same. After full examination, Fraser submitted his report. The Commission criticised the existing Police system forcefully. The Commission indicated:

"The working of police force is not satisfactory. There were lacunas in its training and organisation. Also it did not work properly. It was branded with bribe-taker and causing undue pressures. Neither people had confidence in it nor the public support was available to them. Fraser Commission suggested as under:

1. The existing institutions should be used for imparting training.
2. Well-educated persons should be appointed in police with good carrier prospects.
3. Proper arrangement be made for the training of officers and sepoys and new training schools should be opened.

4. Special watch be kept on personnel of lower ranks.
5. For higher posts, direct recruitment should be made rather than filling these posts by promotion only.
6. The salary of the sepoy should be sufficient to lead a comfortable life and it should be minimum Rs.8 per month.
7. Police force should be increased in each province. The persons doing police job in villages should be enrolled in police. Beat system prevailing in villages be stopped and sepoys should be sent to villages to collect specific information only and in this way their visits to the villages be reduced.
8. The crimes should be examined then and there itself. No one should be detained without formal arrest. Admissions under duress/pressure should not be taken cognizance of. The police work should be measured on the basis of the inspections conducted and investigations made and not simply on statistics.
9. There should be a Criminal Investigation Department in each province under the Central Government and the criminal investigation spying department should be under a Director.

The Government of India accepted the above recommendations but on the implementation of these recommendations, expenditure of police increased to 4602977 in 1911 from 2691344 in 1901-02 but there was no commensurate improvement in police functioning. Still the police was allowed to work on these lines.

Village Policing

In view of the vastness of the territory and difficult terrain, it would have been unrealistic for any ruler to expect that the ruler appointed agencies could ensure safety and security of the people in the country side without adequate participation in the process of the village community. Therefore, in ancient times, the village watchman was a person so designated and maintained by village community in which he lived and his duty was to guard the person and property of the villagers from attacks by dacoits and other criminals. The watchman was a public servant either of rent receiver or of the rent paying villagers, who supported him. During Muslim rule, Zamindars were appointed to collect revenue and to conduct the civil and criminal administration of the area entrusted to such Zamindars. The village watchman was merged into Zamindar establishment. In this way the autonomy of the villages, where village panchayats monitored all civil and criminal cases as per tenets of samritis and followed in the Hindu rulers' period, had been entrusted to one man 'the Zamindar' during Muslim period. Such a Zamindar had become overall Lord of the village and could do anything in the village. He generally harassed the farmers in realising revenues and part of the product to fill up his coffers and in this way the entire village lived at the mercy of the Zamindar losing all the piety available during Vedic period and the rule of Hindu rajas.

The East India Company and subsequent British rulers also realised that effective policing of the country side was not possible through the official policeman. Hence various experiments were tried out in different parts of India to ensure a satisfactory linkage between the criminal justice administration, including Police on one hand and the village community on the other, including village watchmen. The Police Commission of 1902 reviewed village policing and recommended:

1. The responsibility of the village watchman, for the performance of village police duties, should be recognised and enforced in every province and watchman should be a village servant subordinate to village headman and not to the regular police.
2. The supervision and control of the village headmen should be entrusted to the Collector or Deputy Commissioner and his subordinate officers.
3. The regular periodical attendance of village watchmen at the Police Station was unneccessary and undesirable.

4. It was expedient to relegate the trial of petty officers to village headmen and panchayats and that where this system did not exist, it deserved to be introduced experimentally and cautiously.

The Presidency towns of Calcutta, Bombay and Madras were not only the seats of power but also the places, where largest European population in India resided. Hence the policing of three Presidency towns was developed on a different footing compared to the policing of the district towns and country side as in Calcutta. Accordingly:

1. Thanedari Police was introduced dividing town in forty thanas each incharge of a thanedar.
2. Boundary Police were located at twenty-two thanas forming a chain of posts around the towns, each under a jamadar, a naib with 8-16 burkundazes.
3. River Police was formed consisting of a sircar, eighteen peons and nineteen boatmen.
4. Town guards introduced, which were initially composed entirely of sepoys but burkundazes were added later. The force was under town Major and four Sergeants.
5. There was a special guard called 'Uperpusti' or grand rounds consisting of one jamadar, nine naiks and seventy three guards.

Semi military forces had been created by the Government of India from time to time as the requirement arose to control the law and order. The following forces are in existence today:

1. **Assam Rifles**: It was created mainly to control the law and order situation in north eastern India in addition to the local police. It was an armed force.
2. **Border Security Force:** This armed force or semi military force had been created in 1969 to protect India's border with Pakistan, China, Nepal, Bhutan and Burma and to protect India from infiltration of aliens from these countries as also from smugglings across the border.

3. **Central Industrial Special Force**: This is a central police force created in 1969 for assets protection, loss prevention and personnel security in any industry. Initially the sanctioned strength was three battalions comprising of 2000 persons. In 1989, the strength was 71,260.

4. **Central Reserve Police Force**: It was another central police force to assist the State police in cases of bad state of law and order by extremists/terrorists. It was created in 1949 although initially in semblance it was started at Neemuch in Madya Pradesh in 1939 as Central Reserve Police. It is one of the armed forces of the union for purposes of utilisation in riots or disturbances in internal security.

5. **Foreign Intelligence Research and Analysis Wing (RAW)**: Created to collect, through the spies, information of use to this country from the foreign countries.

6. **Indo-Tibetan Border Police**: Set up in 1962 in the wake of Chinese aggression with four Battalions. Subsequently the strength has been increased as per requirement from time to time.

7. **Railway Protection Force**: This force, armed and unarmed, was created for the protection of Railway property and goods handed over to be carried by Railways.

8. **States Criminal Intelligence Department (CIDs)**

9. **Intelligence Bureau**

10. **Special Police Establishment**

For the purpose of this book we will take up States CIDs, Intelligence Bureau, Special Police Establishment in more details.

States CIDs: These were introduced in 1904 with a view to apprehend the persons involved in anti-Government activities. The history of CID takes us back to the institute of Manu, who stipulated that the king must explore by means of spies, both within the States of his own kingdom, the criminals and his enemies. Manu describes five classes of spies in various disguises. The Ramayana too mentions the need for watching through spies. Mahabharata describes spies of Duryodhana reporting to King. But a fairly elaborate system of espionage is found in Kautilya's Arthshastra as already discussed. Kautilya writes of the activities of spies in the Maurya and post Maurya periods. Kautilya says that the king is not to rely upon the report of a single spy. He advocates five institutes of espionage controlling the entire intelligence collection set up for checking and verifying reports received through different sources. The spies, he goes on to say, were to perform different duties. The espionage system continued during the Pathan and Mughal rule. Sir Jagannath in his book on Mughal administration says that espionage system was highly efficient during the reign of Akbar. Akbar used to listen to the spies in confidence in 'Zenana' and 'Khilafat Khana.'

Intelligence Bureau: The history of Intelligence Bureau during the British raj can be traced to a small group of officers and reliable net-work of informers employed by Sir William Sleeman in the suppression of thugee organisation between 1830-1837. The eradication of this menace was largely due to the employment of reliable informers under the overall leadership of Sleeman. The 'Thugee' and 'Dakaiti' department established by Sleeman in 1835 was in effect Criminal Investigation Department concerned mainly with these particular forms of crime. After the mutiny and more specifically with effect from about 1860, the department ceased to have any executive functions. In 1877 under the charge of Col. Hinderson, the general superintendence of the department was given the additional duty of collecting secret and political intelligence. All the modern intelligence collection organisations are a natural development for the new and expanded functions of the 'Thugee' and 'Dacoity' department.

In 1901, Government of India began to consider the formation of a small detective force under the orders of the Inspector General of Police in each province due to the agitations started in Bengal due to the proposal of partition of Bengal, subsequently spread to other provinces as freedom movement. Earlier the Police Commission of 1860 had rejected the idea of a separate detective service and in 1869 also, a proposal of the Chief Commissioners of the Central Provinces for the appointment of separate chief constables for detective work had been turned down by the Government of India on the ground that it would lead to abuse and oppression.

In 1901, the approach of the Government of India to this subject was more positive than it had hitherto been and they recommended that the central special branch should be extended by the addition of a small staff of selected detective agents to be employed in watching political movements and in dealing with those forms of organised crime, which extended beyond the limits of a single province.

In 1904, Government of India proposed the establishment of Central Criminal Intelligence Department to collect and communicate information obtained from the Provincial Criminal Investigation Departments or otherwise and it should include :

(a) Dealing with special form of crime, some of which have been rendered more difficult of suppression by the recent extensions of Railways and the increased use of the Post Office and Telegraphs by natives. Under this, head of department would organise and supervise operations directed against criminal tribes, organised dacoits working over large areas, wandering gangs of criminals, forgers, professional poisoners etc.

(b) Collecting and testing intelligence upon political matters including social, religious, and political movements, not necessarily of a criminal character.

The new organisation came into being in April 1904. In practice the political intelligence work occupied the whole time of the department and its functions in relation to special forms of crime were quietly dropped. For this reason, after the First World War, the name of this department was changed to Intelligence Bureau.

The new organisation was also made responsible for the collection of information required by the Governor General personally, the army, the Agent to Governor General and his political agents and the Governors of neighbouring provinces regarding what was going on in North West Frontier Province, tribal territories, Afghanistan, Sinkiang and parts of USSR adjacent to India. In addition, it will have to provide information regarding subversive activities connected with or directed by Communist International and the intrigues of Ghadar Party emanating from Moscow and other places in Europe and Afghanistan.

By the thirties, the intelligence system in India — both in its political and non-political scope — had been well organised but the inauguration of provincial autonomy in 1937 brought about one important change. The police in each province came under the Minister for Home Affairs, who was responsible for day-to-day administration of law and order. Governor General had his own way of getting information independent of Ministers. The Central Intelligence was also required to make a careful study of press — both English and Vernacular — and to keep in touch with the political organisations.

The Second World War added considerably to the work and responsibility of various intelligence branches and a considerable expansion of their strength was made. The entry of Japan in conflict and their victories in South Asia, activities of Indian National Army (INA), Congress's opposition to war efforts, counter intelligence activities as a result of establishment of Prisoners of War Camps in India, the Quit India Movement — all these events surpassed each other and the intelligence machinery found its hands full.

With independence, India was beset with serious problems such as invasion of Kashmir, integration of Princely States, Hyderabad Police Action, Nagaland and Mizoram problems, Chinese incursions, Punjabi suba and language agitation and terrorism caused all problems for Intelligence Bureau.

The Organisation has grown with the passing of years and continue to guide the national leadership away from catastrophe and is the most effective machinery in the maintenance of internal security of the country. The Intelligence Bureau is also incharge of foreign intelligence.

Special Police Establishment: During World War II, the Government of India realised that the vast increase in expenditure for war efforts had provided opportunities to unscrupulous and anti-social persons—both officials and non-officials—for indulging in bribery and corruption at the cost of the police and the government. It was felt that the police and the law enforcement agencies under State governments were not in a position to cope with the situation. Therefore, to investigate offences connected with transactions relating to war efforts, an organisation known as Special Police Establishment was set up by the Government of India in 1941 under executive order of the Central Government.

The functions of the Special Police Establishment were to investigate cases of bribery and corruption in transactions with which the War and Supply Department of Government of India was concerned and, therefore, the superintendence of this organisation was vested under the War Department. At the end of 1942, the activities of the Special Police Establishment were extended to include cases of corruption on the Railways also presumably because the Railways were vitally concerned with the movement and supply of war materials.

In 1943, an ordinance was issued by the Government of India by which the Special Police Establishment, entrusted with the investigation of certain offences committed in connection with the departments of the central government with powers to investigate such offences anywhere in British India, was constituted. Even after the war, the need for a central government agency to investigate cases of bribery and corruption by central government servants was felt and, therefore, the ordinance issued in 1943 was replaced by Delhi Special Police Establishment Ordinance of 1946, subsequently replaced by Delhi Special Police Establishment Ordinance of 1946. After that the Superintendence of Special Police Establishment was transferred to Home Department and its functions were enlarged to cover all departments of the Government of India. Since then, the Special Police Establishment functions under this Act and its jurisdiction extends to the States with the consent of State governments concerned.

In 1953, Enforcement wing was added to Special Police Establishment to deal with the offences, relating to breach of Import and Export Regulations. This wing, now known as Economic Offences Wing, continues to deal with not only cases of violation of Import and Export Control Act but other fiscal laws of Central Government.

With the passage of time, more and more cases under laws other than Prevention of Corruption Act and violation of Import and Export Control Act also came to be entrusted to Special Police Establishment. A growing need was, therefore, felt for a Central Police Agency at the disposal of the Central Government, which would investigate not only cases of bribery and corruption but also cases of breaches of Central Fiscal Laws, major frauds relating to Government of India departments, Public Joint Stock Companies, passport frauds and, therefore, the Government of India set up the Central Bureau of Investigation (CBI) on April 01, 1963. The Organisation and the functions of the Central Bureau of Investigation are given in Government Resolution of April 01, 1963. The jurisdiction, powers and functions of the Special Police Establishment remained as before even after the setting up of the Central Bureau of Investigation.

Besides investigation of crimes, the CBI was also entrusted with the task of collection of intelligence relating to certain types of crimes, maintenance of crime statistics and dissemination of information relating to crime and criminals, study of specialised form of ramification of crimes of particular importance from the social point of view, the conduct of police research and the coordination of laws. With the setting up of the Bureau of Police Research and Development, functions relating to maintenance of crime statistics and dissemination of information relating to crime and criminals and the conduct of Police research have been transferred to Police Research and Development. However, instead of the original six division of the CBI mentioned in Government Resolution of April 01, 1963, the CBI has now the following eight divisions:

1. Anti Corruption Division
2. Special Crimes Division
3. Legal Division headed by Legal Advisor and having Additional Legal Advisers, Deputy Legal Advisers and Public Prosecutors under him.
4. Technical Division: It provides technical assistance to investigation officers in the scrutiny of records.
5. Policy and Organisation Division.
6. Administration Division.
7. Coordination and Interpol Division: It provides assistance and support to the states in the organisation by way of periodical drives. Interpol Division corresponds to National Central Bureau to elicit information from other countries.
8. Central Forensic Science Laboratory: Situated at Delhi, it caters to the needs of Delhi Police and CBI.

The powers of the Special Police Establishment for investigation of offences notified under Delhi Special Police Establishment Act are not exclusive but concurrent with those of the State Police, and an officer of above the rank of a Sub-inspector of the Special Police Establishemt, is deemed to be an officer incharge of a Police Station, both in Union territories and the States. However, an administrative arrangement had been arrived at between the Central Government and the State Governments about the types of cases to be taken up for investigation by the Special Police Establishment. The arrangement is that:

1. Cases which substantially and essentially concern central government employees or its affairs, even though

involving certain State government employees, shall be taken up by the Special Police Establishment.

2. Cases which substantially involve State government employees or affairs relating to State government even though involving certain Central Government employees shall be taken up by the State Police.

3. The Special Police Establishment is also authorised to take up cases against the employees of statutory bodies or Public Sector Undertakings set up and financed by the Government of India.

The strength of Special Police Establishment, which in 1962 had fifteen branches in State capitals, besides its head office in Delhi and two Central Investigating Units with all India jurisdiction, was substantially increased as a result of the recommendations of the Committee on Prevention of Corruption (Santhanam Committee) and the number of branches was also increased by three.

The CBI organisation, with its headquarters at Delhi, is headed by a Director, assisted by Additional Directors, Joint Directors and DIGs/Deputy Directors. The CBI has branches located at headquarters of most of the State capitals and at Delhi. The CBI's various branches also function from cities other than State capitals i.e. Dhanbad, Jodhpur, Nagpur, Silchar, Ranchi, Dehradun, Jabalpur, Cochin, Visakhapatnam. Sub-units are also located at Guwahati, Izanagar, Imphal, Aizwal, Barmer, Bhuj, Sri Ganganagar, Siliguri, Rourkela, Agartala, Jammu and Shimla.

While retaining its original character of investigating offences involving Central Government and Central Public Sector Undertakings employees, it take up cases of violation of economic and fiscal laws, special crimes of a sensational and complicated nature, terrorists and drugs related crimes, besides taking up cases entrusted by the Supreme Court and High Courts. In particular, the CBI covers the following types of cases:

1. Cases relating to bribery, corruption, misconduct of public servants under the control of the Central Government.

2. Cases in which the interests of the Central Government or of any Public Sector Project or Undertaking or Statutory Corporation set up and financed by the Central Government are involved.
3. Cases of corruption involving senior State Government servants and other important persons, taken up for investigation on the request of the States.
4. Cases of economic offences, including those having international ramifications. Cases relating to essential commodities, customs, central excise, income tax, Foreign Exchange Regulations and Import and Export Act falling in this category.
5. Cases of conventional crimes such as murders, rapes, dowry deaths referred by Central or State Governments.
6. Frauds in Banks, Insurance Companies, Joint Stock Companies.
7. Cases pertaining to Special Act, Arms Act, Official Secrets Act and Special Crimes pertaining to antique thefts, counterfeit of currency and bank notes, unauthorised infiltration of foreigners and espionage activities.
8. Cases against terrorists.
9. Cases which are entrusted by the Supreme Court or the High Courts.
10. Offences against women referred by the Central/State governments and Supreme Court/High Courts.
11. To elicit information desired or judicial assistance required from any country and exchanging intelligence about international smuggling and trafficking in gold, drugs.

Thus the CBI's conceptual role of mainly an anti-corruption agency has undergone radical transformation. The CBI (Special Police Establishment) is now authorised to investigate offences under 191 different sections of the I.P.C. and 55 Central Acts.

(The figures given, get on changing from time to time based on requirement).

8 CONCLUSION

From the narration given so far, it would be clear that the CBI or investigation/spying system has been in vogue in India almost eversince the advent of mankind and there has been a continuous evolution in the same suiting to requirements from time to time as enumerated below:

1. After the man came in society, the question of protection of life cropped up and so a king was appointed for this purpose. He created a force to protect the people from outside aggressions and the internal crime. Initially it was a common force for dealing with external aggressions, internal crime, the detection and punishment of criminals, as also the spying job with a view to keep the king posted with information of what had been happening in the State.

2. There is special mention in Vedas about separate departments existing for spying, vigilance and maintenance of law and order.

3. During Ramayana period, the spies were in existence and the king also used to go incognito to know for himself the happenings in the kingdom.

4. During Krishna period and Mahabharata also, Kansa and Duryodhana are said to be having their spies. Through spies only, Kansa desired to kill Krishna while in Gokul.

5. Although Hindu kings in ancient period were aware of such institutions but lack of spying system with Raja Porus and efficient spying system with Alexander is apparent, leading to defeat of Raja Porus.

6. During Maurya period, the spying system was in existence at its peak and there is detailed narration of the same

in Kautilya's Arthshastra. It is mostly because of the efficient spying system working in his kingdom and in the kingdom of other kings that Mauryas could build the vastest kingdom ever had by any king in India. Ashoka though benevolent ruler yet paid due attention to spying system and severe punishment was awarded to criminals detected by them.

7. During Kanishka's time too Arthshastra was followed.
8. During Gupta period again a strong spying system and proper law and order maintenance was adhered to leading to Fahien saying that there was no crime in that regime. Samudra Guptas too had conquered entire northern and southern India; Southern India having been retained as vassal states; and such a vast empire, including the vassal states, could be managed with a strong spying system only.
9. The administration had continued to be managed with the tenets of Arthshastra during Harsha's time although by then there had been some lawlessness as narrated by Hiuen Tsang as compared to the Gupta period but still it was kept under control.
10. There had been slackness in spying system during the Rajputs period resulting in the defeat at the hands of Muslim invaders. The Rajput rulers were caught unawares by Mahmud Ghazni, who invaded India seventeen time and could go as deep in the country as Somnath temple and went with huge booty. Subsequently, although Mohammed Ghori had been defeated several times by Indian rulers, he was ultimately successful in defeating Prithvi Raj, when he was caught unawares, again due to the lack of spying system with him.
11. In Sultanates, Balban could manage his kingdom crimeless with the help of a net of spies. He had finished all robbers and dacoits and no chief or king could rise in rebellion against him due to his vast spies organisation and proper policing of villages, towns, high-ways and due to the introduction of the system of news-writers, news-carriers

and reporters and police chowkies in villages, towns and high-ways.

12. In Khiljis, Ala-ud-din Khilji again strengthened his spying system, news-writers' and news-carriers' organisation and proper policing of the entire area, strong enough to eliminate crime and foreign aggressions/rebellions by other chiefs/rajas.

13. During the period of Mohammed Tughlaq, the spying had become slack due to which the token currency system introduced by him failed. He also failed on several other fronts due to lack of receipt of information about what had been happening in the kingdom.

14. During Lodhi period, Sikander Lodhi had given importance to proper spying system, law and order enforcing machinery and the organisation for carriage of news. But then Ibrahim ignored these organisations and was defeated by Babar on invitation of his uncle, who was Chief of Punjab.

15. Humayun was defeated by Sher Shah Suri because of lack of receipt of information by him through his spies and Sher Shah working on a very strong spying system. He could check up the position and attack with surprise and suddenly. He kept this up during his reign too.

16. Akbar had made strong spying system. He had been going incognito visiting the kingdom. He also heard the spies specially in 'Khilafat Khana' and 'Zenana', where none else could go. It was only because of a strong spying/policing system that he managed the kingdom very efficiently and Mughal rule continued for over two centuries.

17. During Aurangzeb's time, the kingdom had become very vast and he could not manage such a vast kingdom from centralised government. This could have been possible if proper watch was kept on all chiefs/governors through spies and made them feel that they were all being watched by the emperor.

18. After Aurangzeb, the Mughal empire started dwindling

and because of the lack of receipt of information from chiefs/governors, who had all declared themselves independent and lack of action taken against them that the Mughal empire became shorter and shorter so much so that Bahadur Shah had only a few districts in and around Delhi, in his kingdom.

19. Shivaji had great spying system. He could rise from the scratch only by dint of efficient spies, who used to give him correct and timely information about the enemy, after which only Shivaji would attack. This is how he killed Afzal Khan; defeated Shayasta Khan, came out from the prison of Aurangzeb; got money by robbing from government treasuries/chests; and ultimately founded a Hindu kingdom during Mughal regime itself, when no Hindu could even think of the same. Subsequently too he had been a successful ruler because of a net of spies in his kingdom, who would apprise him of what had been happening in the entire country.

20. Ranjit Singh too became a ruler to be reckoned at that time because he would invade the neighbouring Chief/Nawab after knowing the position of his force, weak points and thus became victorious. His kingdom had been very strong and even British were afraid of touching him. Even after the death of Ranjit Singh, the Sikh army had several times almost defeated the British but just when the Sikh army was likely to win, British, through their secret treacherous methods, purchased the Commander to his side resulting in the defeat ofz Sikhs. Gulab Singh, Lal Singh, Teja Singh are such examples, who thus managed to get the Sikh army defeated.

21. So far as the British are concerned, they could become rulers of the country because of their efficient spying system, treacherous activities by bribing the commanders and subsequently controlled the empire by efficient spying system and after introduction of proper police system in the country.

22. At first we notice it in the battle of Plassy, when Aminchand and Jagat Seth had been engaged by the

British to prepare a plot to get Siraj-ud-daula defeated by Mir Jafar surrendering during the battle on consideration of his being made Governor of Bengal. They charged heavily from the British for such a plot. Siraj-ud-daula could not know of the movement of British company bringing the armeda from Madras to fight with Siraj and subsequent preparations, which resulted in the battle with Siraj; surrender of Mir Jafar and consequent defeat of Siraj and foundation of British rule in India.

23. In battle of Buxar, the Mughal emperor helped British against Shah Alam, Nawab of Oudh and Mir Qasim, resulting in victory of British army.

24. East India Company used to post their Residents in the territories they won. These Residents used to work as spies for the Company in those kingdoms and protected British interest.

25. East India Company introduced Subsidiary System, according to which the Company maintained some army at the cost of the kingdoms and this army was used by British in case of need. Similarly some army was kept by the kingdoms, which could also be used by British in case of need. All these troops worked as spies for British in Indian States.

26. In First War of Mysore, Haider Ali attacked British in corroboration with Nizam but Nizam also had alliance with British and in this way Haider Ali was defeated. Later on British and Nizam entered into a treaty.

27. Under Permanent Settlement of Bengal of 1793, British created a class of Zamindars in Bengal, which always took care to look into British interest in the State.

28. In fourth Mysor war of 1789, Tipu Sultan wanted to take revenge from British in alliance with Nizam. British came to know of the planning through their spies and they had alliance with Nizam, defeating Tipu Sultan.

29. Marathas were not united. The main kings were Scindhia, Holkar, Gaikwar and Bhonsle. Scindhia and Holkar had dispute within themselves. Peshwa helped Scindhia but

Holkar defeated Scindhia and Peshwa in an attack. Peshwa asked for British help and a Treaty of Bassien was entered into after Second War of Marathas in 1802-04. According to this treaty, Peshwa agreed to keep British army in Poona at their expenses and in this way British got control over Marathas as a result of which Marathas could never rise again.

30. Again in Third War of Marathas, they were defeated by British. The main reason for this defeat was spying system of British. They learned Marathi language and started remitting information about the Marathas movement to the Company. In this way, British defeated them for good.

31. British entered into a treaty with Amir of Sind that Amir of Sind would not appoint French in his army and British would not be allowed to cross Sind with their army. But British did not act according to this treaty and took their army through Sind in Afghan war. On checking by Amir of Sind, he was threatened with war and snatched a lot of wealth from him. During entire Afghan war, British had made Sind as their base and later on after the battle, Sind was annexed in British territory.

32. After Ranjit Singh's death, first Sikh war with British took place in 1845, when Sikhs had been fighting for succession to throne. Army had their say in the matter. At the same time, having not been able to control the army, Rani Janda and Lal Singh ordered army to march on British with the intention that in case army won, they would be overall lord of British territory and if they lose, the army would lose their say in the war of succession. Sikh army crossed Satlej and attacked on British army. When Sikh army was likely to win, Lal Singh had alliance with British and so Sikhs were defeated. Again when in second Sikh war, Sikhs were likely to win, Teja Singh had alliance with British resulting in the defeat of Sikhs. Then Gulab Singh became Commander-in-Chief but he too for personal gain plotted with British to make Sikh army defeated. It was agreed that British army would attack on Sikh army and on the latter's defeat, Gulab

Singh would be made king of Kashmir. In the battle, at first Teja Singh fled away followed by Gulab Singh. In this way, because of the treacherous activities of British, a very strong Khalsa army had been suppressed and Punjab had been annexed into British territory.

33. At the time of 1857 Mutiny, the spies and Residents of English Company were spread in entire India and from there, they got information of movements at all places. On the rebellion by Meerut army, British called in army from Bombay, Madras and Bengal because they had known from their spies that there was no rebellion in those provinces. With this army, British could quell the rebellion by Nana Sahib, Rani Jhansi, Nawab Oudh. In Delhi, Sikh army also helped British in subduing the rebels. Later on, all, who were responsible for the rebellion were traced and hanged, and terror was spread in the country so that no one could dare rebel again. British moved the army after checking up the position of each province. Many Hindu and Muslim chiefs also helped British. As a result of the suppression of Mutiny in 1857, British could rule over India further for 90 years.

34. After 1857, British stopped further annexations and over 300 States came into being. They had autonomy for internal administration but external affairs and defence were in British hands. There were British Ambassadors in each State. These Ambassadors kept British apprised of all that had been happening in the States. This infact is the purpose of posting Ambassadors in other countries too so that they may inform their governments of what had been happening in those countries and to keep a watch on their countries' interest in the foreign countries. Any spying by Embassy staff in other countries is forbidden by international law but this is what is happening and on apprehension of such persons spying in that country, the country to which they belong to, is asked to recall them.

35. After 1857, there was calm in the country for about three decades when Indian National Congress came on the scene. The British, with the help of their spies, caught

the congressmen, who indulged in violations. At first the congress had been peaceful, but the partition of Bengal put violative temperament in the people, which initially limited to Bengal, spread to other parts of the country in the form of extremists. For suppressing extremists, who boycotted British products and preached for swadeshi use, violence was caused particularly when students too joined the movement. Subsequently, this forum came out to demand independence for India. The freedom fighters had been imprisoned, time and again, and they were apprehended and their activities were kept under surveillance by the spies of Intelligence Department. This continued till independence in 1947.

RESOLUTION

The Government of India have had under consideration the establishment of a Central Bureau of Investigation for the investigation of crimes at present handled by the Delhi Special Police Establishment including specially important cases under the Defence of India Act and Rules particularly of hoarding, black marketing and profiteering in essential commodities, which may have repurcussions and ramifications in several States, the collection of intelligence relating to certain types of crime participation in the work of the National Central Bureau in connection with the International Criminal Police Organisation; the maintenance of crime statistics and dissemination of information relating to crime and criminals, the study of specialised crime of particular interest to the Government of India or crimes having all India or inter-state ramifications or of a particular importance from the social point of view; the conduct of police research, and the coordination of laws relating to crime. As a first step in that direction, the Government of India have decided to set up with effect from 1st April 1963, a Central Bureau of Investigation at Delhi with the following six Divisions viz.

1. Investigation and anti corruption Division.
2. Technical Division.
3. Crime Records and Statistics Division.
4. Research Division.
5. Legal Division and General Division.
6. Administration Division.

The character of functions of the above said Divisions will be as given in the annexure. The assistance of the Central Bureau of Investigation will also be available to the State police forces on request for investigation and assisting in the investigation of inter-state crime and other difficult criminal cases.

Sd. V. Viswanathan
Secretary to the Government of India
01.04.1963

ANNEXURES

(A) Investigation and Anti-Corruption Division (DSPE)

(i) Cases in which public servants under the control of the Central Government are involved either by themselves or along with State Government servants and/or other persons.

(ii) Cases in which the interests of the Central Government or of any public sector project or undertaking or any statutory corporation or body set up and financed by the Government of India are involved.

(iii) Cases relating to breaches of central laws with the enforcement of which the Government of India is particularly concerned e.g.

(a) Breaches of Import and Export Control Orders.

(b) Serious breaches of Foreign Exchange Regulations Act.

(c) Passport frauds.

(d) Cases under the Official Secrets Act pertaining to the affairs of the Central Government.

(g) Cases of certain specified categories under the Defence of India Act or Rules with which the Central Government is particularly concerned.

(iv) Serious cases of fraud or cheating relating to the Railways or Posts and Telegraphs Department, particularly those involving professional criminals operating in several states.

(v) Crimes on the high seas.

(vi) Crimes on the Airlines.

(vii) Important and serious cases in Union territories particularly those by professional criminals.

(viii) Serious cases of fraud, cheating and embezzlement relating to Joint Stock Companies.

(ix) Other cases of a serious nature, when committed by organised gangs or professional criminals or cases having ramifications in several States, including Union territories, serious cases of spurious drugs, important cases of kidnappings. Cases will be taken up only at the request of/ or with the concurrence of the State governments /Union Territories Administrations concerned.

(x) Collection of intelligence about corruption in the public services and the projects and undertakings in the public sector.

(xi) Prosecution of cases investigated by this Division.

(xii) Presentation of cases before Enquiry Officers in which departmental proceedings are instituted on the recommendation of the Division.

(B) Technical Division

(1) Technical assistance in investigation of cases involving accounts.

(2) Specialised assistance in cases involving Railways and Postal accounts.

(3) Assistance in cases involving assessment of income tax, excise duty etc.

(4) Examination of accounts and assets in cases relating to allegations of disproportional assets.

(5) Examination of cases investigated by the Bureau, which have an income tax aspect, and communication of information with a view to enabling the Income Tax department to recover the evaded tax.

(C) Crime Records and Statistics Division

1. Maintenance of All India Statistics of crime.
2. Study of all India trends in thefts and losses and recoveries of fire-arms and ammunition and notes forgery and counterfeiting coining.
3. Collection and dissemination of information about important inter-State criminals.
4. Preparation and circulation of reports and reviews relating to crime in India.
5. Participation in the work of the ICPO/NCB/UNO reporter for crime.

(D) Research Division

Analysis and study of specialised crimes and of problems of specialised crimes and of problems of a general nature affecting the police e.g.

1. Trends and causes of serious crimes in different areas.
2. Preventive measures, their effectiveness, and relationship with crime.
3. Improvement in methods of investigations, utility and results of introducing scientific aids and equipments.
4. Inadequacy of laws, coordination of laws relating to crime in various States.
5. Criminal gangs operating in more than one State wandering gangs, ex-criminals, tribes and habitual offenders.
6. Crimes amongst the tribal people.
7. Inter-State notes forgery and counterfeiting.
8. Social factors in crime.
9. Industrialisation and crime.
10. Juvenile delinquency.
11. Kidnapping of women and children.

(E) Legal and General Division

(a) Legal Section

1. Legal advice in cases investigated by the Investigation and Anti Corruption Division;
2. Conducting prosecution in important cases;
3. Review of judicial Decisions relating to criminal law and procedure for publication in the CBI Gazette;
4. Compilation and circulation of Law digests;
5. Inadequacy and amendments to laws; and
6. Coordination of laws relating to crime in various States.

(b) General Section

1. Matters relating to organisation, policy and procedure;
2. Inter-State conference relating to crime and anti-corruption work;
3. Appreciation reports regarding modes of corruption in various government departments and public undertakings;
4. Correspondence with Ministries and States on general questions relating to policy procedure etc.;
5. Training courses in anti-corruption works;
6. CBI Gazette; and
7. Photographic Section.

(F) Administration Division

All establishment and accounts matters.

GLOSSARY

Agni : God of Hindus/Fire

Amins : Land Revenue Collector

Annawala : Names of Kutsa, Minister for Vigilance

Apsaras : Divine Dancers

Ashram : Hermitage

Asura : Demon

Atithigava : Names of Kutsa, Minister for Vigilance

Ayu : Names of Kutsa, Minister for Vigilance

Ayukta : Commissioners

Bakshi : A military officer-in-charge of payments of salaries

Bazars : Markets

Bhagwan : God

Bhakti : Devotion

Booty : Plant/Ayurvedic Medicine

Brahmin : First of four varnas in Hindus

Chief Shiqdar : Police Commissioner

Chirharan : Removal of clothes from body

Chowkies : Posts

Dak : Postal

Dand : Punishment

Dandanayaka : Chief Judge

Dandi Sadhu : Ascetic

Darbar : Court

Daroga : Police Inspector

Darshan : Sight

Dastak : Warrent

Dewane-Riyasat : Minister of State

Dharma : Religion

Dhanushban : Bow and arrow

Dharamyudha : Religious war

Dharmsthana : Religious place

Diwan : Chief Minister

Farmans : Orders

Fauzdars : An officer invested with the charge of the police and had jurisdiction on all criminal matters

Gopa : Village Head

Gram Mukhiya : Village Head

Gwala : Cattle grazer

Harkaras : Messengers

Indra : God of Hindus

Jagirdar : Holders of a jagir

Jyotish : Astrology

Kshatriya : Second of the four varnas in Hindus

Khilawat Khana : A meeting place with ministers by Mughal Kings

Khufiya-navis : Spy

Kiskindhaya : A State ruled by Sugreeva

Kose : Distance of about 1.5 miles

Kottapal : Municipal Commissioner

Kotwals : Police Inspectors

Kuber : God of Hindus

Kumar-matya : Governor

Kutsa : A God incharge of vigilance department

Lakshagriha : A house made of lac

Mahal : Palace

Mahapratiharas : Commissioner

Mamalik : Magistrate

Melas : Fairs

Mufti : Free of cost

Mukhiya : Chief

Munis : Ascetics/Hermits

Munsif : Magistrate

Nagar Rakshadhikrita : Municipal Commissioner

Nagrikas : Citizens

Panchayat : Village council

Phansidar : A tribe which used to rob and kill people

Pradhan : Head of a Village

Praja : Subjects

Pratihara : Collectors

Raja : King

Rajdharma : Duties of the king

Rajmahal : King's Palace

Rakshas : Demon

Rambhakta : Devotee of God Ram

Ram rajya : Reign of God Ram

Razeenama : Agreement

Rishis : Saints

Sadar Diwani : Highest court of civil justice

Sadar Nizamat : Highest criminal court

Sainiks : Soliders

Samharta : Collector

Samritis : Hindu religious books

Sanjeevani booty : Ayurvedic medicinal plant

Sanyasis : Saints

Sarais : Lodges

Sardars : Chieftains

Sarkar : Government

Sarthy : A Charioteer

Satee : Dying with the husband

Shahane-Mandi : Market Officer

Shiqdar : Incharge of revenue collection as well as of maintaining law and order in a Pargana

Shudra : Fourth of the four varnas in Hindus

Soma : Minister for Judiciary

Sthanikas : Religious places

Susarvas : Names of Kutsa, Minister for Vigilance

Swadeshi : Indigenous

Swayamber Choice by bride of her husband

Tapasavi : Ascetic

Tapasya : Asceticism

Thana : Police Station

Thanedar : Commander of one or more check-points ; an incharge of a police station

Thugee : Act of a cheating

Thugs : Cheats

Turvayan : Names of Kutsa, Minister for Vigilance

Upayukta : Deputy Commissioner

Vaish : Third of the four varnas in Hindus

Vanaras : Monkeys

Vanprasthis : Ascetic

Varuna : God of Hindus

Vedas : Hindu religious books

Waqa-navis : Reporter

Yogis : Hermits

Yuvraj : Successor to Throne

Zenana : Emperor's meeting place with his spies

Zamindar : Holder of the Land

INDEX

Afzal Khan, 71

Akbar, 69, 93,103

Alexander, 38-39

Ambi, 38-39

Amin Chand, 74, 83, 104

Arthashastra, 39-50, 54-56, 61, 93, 102

Spies in, 40-42

Ashoka, 49, 51

Assam Rifles, 91

Atharva Veda, 8

Aurangzeb, 71, 73, 103

Babar, 65, 103

Bain, 32

Balban, 60-62, 102

Bana, 55

Bentinck, 78, 80-81

Border Security Force, 91

CBI, 6, 17, 31, 97-101

Chanakya, 39-40, 50, 54, 93, 102

Chandra Gupta, 52, 55

Chandra Gupta Maurya, 39, 49

CISF, 92

Clive, 79

Cornwallis, 75, 78-79

Criminal Procedure Code, 8

CRPF, 92

East India Company, 66, 85, 90, 105, 107

Fahien, 52

Fateh Khan, 64

Fraser Commission, 88

Ghayas-ud-din Tughlaq, 63

Gulab Singh, 84, 104, 106, 107

Haidar Ali, 84, 105

Harappan Civilization, 6

Harish Chandra, 17

Harsha, 55-57

Hastings, 74-75

Hinderson, 93

Hiuen Tsang, 55

Humayun, 65, 68, 103

IB, 92-96

Ibrahim Lodhi, 65, 103

Indian Penal Code, 8

ITBP, 92

Jagat Seth, 74, 104

Jahangir, 73, 76

Jai Chand, 59, 74

Jai Singh, 71

Kalidasa, 54

Kanishka, 51

Katyayan Samriti, 56

Kautilya, 39-40, 50, 54, 93, 102

Krishna Period, 31-37, 101

Kutsa, 11-12

Lal Singh, 84, 104, 106

Lawrence, John, 85

Mahabharata, 38, 50

Mahmud Ghazni, 102
Manu's Police, 53-54
Megasthanese, 50
Mir Jafar, 73-74, 83
Mir Qasim, 74
Mohammed Ghori, 59
Mohammed Tughlaq, 63, 103

Nana Sahib, 107
Narad, 17-18
Narad Samriti, 56-57

Outram, 82

Police Act of 1861, 88
Porus, 38-39
Prithu, 32
Prithvi Raj, 59

Qutab-ud-din Aibak, 60

Ramayana Period, 17-30, 101
Ramcharitmanas, 18, 31
Rani Jhansi, 107
Rani Jinda, 84, 104, 106
Ranjit Singh, 84, 104, 106
RAW, 92
Rigveda, 9-11, 14
Robinson, 86
RPF, 92

Samudra Gupta, 52-53, 102
Seleucus, 39
Shah Alam, 74, 105
Shah Jahan, 73
Sher Shah, 65-67, 103
Shivaji, 71-72, 84, 104
Sikandar Lodhi, 64-65, 103
Sirajuddaula, 73, 105
Sleeman, 81, 93
Soma as minister for Judiciary, 15-16
Srimad Bhagwat, 31-32
Sudraka, 54

Teja Singh, 84, 104, 106-107
Timur, 64
Tipu Sultan, 84

Varuna as Policeman, 6-8
Vedic Period, 6-16
Vishwamitra, 17

Western Police Organisation, 6
World War, First, 94
World War, Second, 96